the
HOLY SPIRIT
and you

Jack Armstrong

JL van Schaik
RELIGIOUS BOOKS

Published by J L van Schaik Publishers
1064 Arcadia Street, Hatfield, Pretoria
All rights reserved
Copyright © 1998 Jack Armstrong

First edition 1998
ISBN 0 627 02378 9

Cover design by Brightmark
Typesetting in 11 $\frac{1}{2}$ on 14 $\frac{1}{2}$ pt Palatino by
Sonja Reinecke, Studio S
Printed and bound by National Book Printers,
Drukkery Street, Goodwood, Western Cape

CONTENTS

FOREWORD

Dr Justin Michell, M.A., D.Phil.

This book will be warmly welcomed by all who long for a closer walk with God, especially those who do not believe that tongues are the only sign of being filled with the Holy Spirit.

Speaking at a Theological Conference recently, Professor B. Engelbrecht said: 'Theology today has nothing of greater importance on its agenda than a careful and comprehensive elaboration of the doctrine of the Holy Spirit."

How true this is, but without doubt we also need to hear from those who, in their own lives, have experienced the glorious renewal that comes with the filling of the Holy Spirit. This book is from the pen of such a person.

Throughout the world there is an increasing conviction that the Church must either be revived or perish. The Lord Jesus assured us, however, that the gates of hell shall not prevail against the Church, the body of Christ. It is therefore not surprising that evidences of revival are to be seen in the Churches in many parts of the world. Sadly enough, some of those who have looked for this renewal, resist it when it comes. The same thing occurred among most of the Jews when the Messiah came.

The author, Jack Armstrong, is a man with a faith that is natural and childlike, yet vigorous and victorious. These qualities, together with his irrepressible smile, combine to make him someone whose book one feels one simply must read. Nor will one be disappointed, for here he shares insights which can only have been given him by the Lord.

The list of contents shows at a glance the eminently practical matters dealt with. These are subjects that Christians all over the world are exploring and this book will assist them in their quest for a clearer understanding of these things and a fuller experience of the Holy Spirit in their lives.

May God bless the content of these chapters richly in your life.

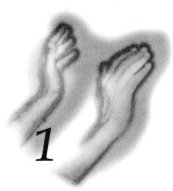

What you picture is what you believe

For whom is this book written? It is written as the Scripture says, "To the Jew first but also to the Greek," or to Gentiles like me *(Rom 2:10)*. I hope that many Jews will read it and not be offended at the name Jesus, for He is our true Messiah.

It is written to the youngest believer, but has much to challenge the profound theologian. It is written for the non-charismatic, but also for the charismatic. It is written for those searching for truth, but also for those who have the truth. It is written for the Pentecostal and non-Pentecostal. It is written for the Catholic and the Protestant.

Why was this book written? It was written to give a clear picture of the Holy Spirit and how He works in our lives. A scripture that sums this up is *1 Corinthians 2:12*: "We have not received the spirit of the world but the Spirit Who is from God, that we may understand what God has freely given us." The picture you create of the **Holy Spirit** is going to be what you believe! This book was written because God told me to write it. God spoke to me while I was driving up and round the hairpin bends of Magoebaskloof, one of South Africa's spectacular mountain passes, set in the superb scenery of virgin forest and man-made plantations of pine and bluegum, of natural lakes and those made by man.

God said: "I will give you what to write. Be strong and of good courage and do it. If you do not do it, I will have to find someone else." I said: "Lord, if You will give me what to write, I will do it. What must the book be about?" The Lord replied, "It shall be the truth about my Holy Spirit. About what I have already taught you and what I shall teach you. It will be written so that my children throughout the world will be able to share their views about the Holy Spirit, and cease to argue about Him. It will be written so that what has been controversial will be made clear. It will be written so that my children may be brought to a oneness and a unity, which is what my Son prayed for in *John 17:21*."

God continued: "This is the supreme reason why you, as my children, have been placed in the world. Not to emphasise division, but to prove to the world that you love Me and that because you love Me you love one another. Different denominations will remain, but you will meet together in great gatherings to demonstrate your oneness to the world. Your unity will be in My Son, the Messiah. Your love will transcend all human love, for it will issue forth from My Holy Spirit Who will flood your hearts with the love of a Father God Who first loved you."

These words seemed to come from my inner being, penetrating my natural thought pattern.

What is the mental picture you hold in your mind of God?

What you picture in your mind will be what you believe. Everyone has a picture of God. Even now thoughts begin to form a picture in your mind, which can be either good or bad, accurate or inaccurate, founded on God's Word, or just what you imagine God to be. It affects our entire lives. We may not think so, yet it does. Even an atheist pictures God, even if he pictures that He does not exist.

You may say my picture of God has nothing to do with what I am, but this is not so. You tend to become like the image of God that you hold in your heart.

If we see God as distant, uncommunicative, indifferent or unsympathetic towards us, all these negative qualities will show up in us. A strong, positive faith cannot find a hold in such a person. To carry this further: If your concept of God is that He wants to whip us into submission, we will be defiant. If it is that He is harsh, angry and punitive, we shall also have an attitude of vengeance. If you see Him as unconcerned with your needs, you will also be unconcerned with the needs of others. You will be unable to put someone else first, unless you can gain by the situation. With such an attitude, God will hardly exist in your life. He will not be in your moment-by-moment consciousness.

Now I am not saying it is wrong to be strong-willed and ambitious. God requires these qualities of us. What I will say is, give your strong will and ambition over to God for Him to direct, then you will really begin to see things happen.

Of course, our concept of God may not be quite as bad as that portrayed above. In your heart of hearts you really love God. You just feel that He is unwilling always to forgive you, that He is a little inconsistent in your case.

You see Him as always attending to the needs of others before your own. He showers His love on others, but not on you.

Now be honest with yourself. If you carry this picture of God, you will see that it is impossible to give yourself fully and wholly, to a God you do not respect. This produces a lack of fulfilment in most people; even an inward struggle. It results in physical, psychological and spiritual problems.

"What can I do?" you ask, "I can't help being the way I am!" Well, you can by asking yourself whether your concept of God is correct. We must get the foundation right. God's image in our minds must be what He tells us in his Word, not what we imagine Him to be. As we learn of God through his Word, and while we trust the Holy Spirit to teach us, we receive increasing revelation of Him as He truly is. At the same time, our born-again spirit blossoms forth *(1 Jn 2:20, 26, 27; John 14:26; Eph 1:17–20)*. As we yield to God, his Spirit begins to change and mould our personalities and characters, something we cannot do ourselves.

If we have a wrong picture of the Holy Spirit, what we believe about Him will also be wrong. If we have a true biblical, God-given picture of the Holy Spirit, this is what we are going to believe. If we have a hazy picture of the Holy Spirit, our experience of the Holy Spirit will also be hazy.

The aim of this book is to give a clear, scriptural picture of the Holy Spirit in our lives. What we ultimately picture with our minds is going to be what we believe.

When I have asked well-established Christians how they picture God, how they picture the Holy Spirit, I have been shocked at the unscriptural images people have. No wonder many do not come to know Him intimately and never hear Him speak to them.

Someone told me: "I picture God as a ball of light. He is like a bright, round cloud. Underneath, the cloud is dark. This begins to drop down like rain. This rain is the Holy Spirit."

If the Holy Spirit was a Person whom he knew and could talk to, he would not talk about God as a ball of light, and the Holy Spirit proceeding from the dark side of God like rain.

The way to picture God is first to know Jesus. In *John 14:5–9* we read: "Thomas said unto Him, 'Lord, we don't know where you are going, so how can we know the way?' Jesus answered, 'I am the way and the truth and the life. No one comes to the Father except through Me. If you really knew Me, you would know my Father as well. From now on, you do know Him (the Father) and have seen Him.'"

"Philip said, 'Lord, show us the Father and that will be enough for us.'

Jesus answered, 'Don't you know Me, Philip, even after I have been among you for such a long time? Anyone who has seen Me has seen the Father.'"

The matter is quite simple, really. Jesus has a body just like ours. It is easy to picture Him. He came to reveal our Heavenly Father to us. Jesus says if we have seen Him, we have seen the Father. The Father has a body – a spiritual body – in appearance similar to that of Jesus after his resurrection, but without flesh and bones like Jesus has. The Father is so much more majestic that, until we receive our new changed, immortal bodies which we read about in *1 Corinthians 15:50–52*, we could not see the Father and live *(Exod 33:20)*.

A beautiful description of God is given in *Ezekiel 1:26–28*, extracts of which I quote here: "High above on the throne was a figure like that of a Man. I saw that from what appeared to be the waist up He looked like glowing metal, as if full of fire, and that from there down He looked like fire; and brilliant light surrounded Him like the appearance of a rainbow in the clouds on a rainy day, so was the radiance around Him. This was the appearance of the likeness of the Glory of the *Lord*."

Isn't this a magnificent picture of our Father in heaven? Picture Him there! Who is seated at His right hand? Jesus! *(Eph 1:20, 2:6)*. We are the body of Christ, *(Eph 5:23)* and "Christ Jesus ... is at the right hand of God ... interceding for us ..." *(Rom 8:34)* to make us "more than conquerors" (v. 37).

What is our relationship with Jesus?

Jesus, interceding for us, his church, prayed in *John 17:21–23*, "That all of them (his children) may be one, Father, just as you are in Me and I am in You. May they also be in us so that (the people in) the world may believe You sent Me. I have given them the glory that You gave Me, that they may be one as we are one ... May they be brought to complete unity to let the world know that You sent Me and (that You) have loved them even as You have loved Me."

Our Father loves us as much as He does Jesus! Let us in an act of faith believe this and thank Him for this kind of love. At the same time, let us by faith recognise that Jesus said that He has given us: "The glory that the Father gave Him." By our faith, we appropriate this glory and are clothed with it as we walk through this life and thank Him for the reality in our ordinary lives.

What does the Holy Spirit do?

2 Corinthians 1:22 says that our Loving Father "Set His seal of ownership on us and put His Spirit in our hearts as a deposit, guaranteeing what is to come." In *Romans 8:16* we read that "The Holy Spirit Himself testifies with our spirit that we are God's children" and in verse 26 that "The Spirit helps us in our weakness" and "The Spirit intercedes for us in accordance with God's will."

John 14:26 proclaims that "The Counsellor the Holy Spirit ... will teach you all things" and *John 16:13* that "The Spirit of truth ... will guide you into all the truth." The Holy Spirit does not have a body, so He indwells us to do all this for us. Isn't it wonderful how the Father, Son and Holy Spirit are all for us, encouraging us and loving us?

How do we approach our Father?

Hebrews 4:16 (King James version) says, "Let us therefore come boldly unto the throne of grace." Jesus said we must just use his name when we approach our Father: "In that day you will no longer ask Me anything. I tell you the truth, My Father will give you whatever you ask in My Name ... Ask and You will receive, and your joy will be complete" *(John 16:23–24)*. God cannot lie, so I believe you must change any wrongful ideas about God. God is a good God and the devil is a bad devil. Good things come to me from God and bad things come to me from the devil.

Where my picture of God has been wrong I want it corrected. Don't you? And why should this be? Because what I picture about God is going to determine what I believe!

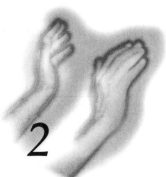

You have given your life to Christ. What now?

2

Our pastor, Reverend Edmund Roebert, asked the following question at the mid-week Bible Study with about 500 people of all ages present: What advice would you give to a new Christian who is just starting out in the Christian life?

Quick as a flash people responded:

"You must start an early quiet time."

"Learn how to pray; read your Bible; start in the New Testament."

"Experience sanctification."

"Live a life of repentance."

"Be baptised."

"Live a holy life."

"Attend the prayer meeting."

"Come to the Bible Study."

"Have fellowship with other Christians."

"Let the love of Christ flow from you."

"Attend the Church services on Sundays."

"Stop swearing!"

Someone read portions of *Hebrews 6:1–2* (KJ) "Let us go on to perfection ... repentance of dead works ... have faith toward God. The doctrine of baptisms and laying on of hands, and of the resurrection of the dead." The person continued with verse 11: "That you show diligence to the full assurance of hope unto the end." and verse 12: "That you be not slothful, but be followers of them who through faith and patience inherit the promises."

"Start witnessing," said another.

These are the actual answers people gave. I copied them down as the various people suggested them! Well, this new Christian certainly got bombarded! I wonder if he might not be so overwhelmed that he thinks he might as well give up before he has started.

Let's say you find someone who does not have this reaction. He is determined to do everything expected of him as above and manages to do it all. Yet, the person who gave the good advice to do all the things listed above, did not tell him how to let the love of God flow from him.

After three months our new Christian gets some satisfaction from the fact that he is accomplishing something. Everyone says, "What a transformation! Here is a Christian on the ball!"

He manages for a year. Then tragedy begins to strike. Now the initial enthusiasm is wearing off. To himself he says, "No one else will know if I don't get up so early to pray. I think I know enough of the Bible now, I'll stop reading, but so that others don't know, I'll take my Bible to church. No one will find out that I am not reading it anymore."

I began to ask myself, and God, what was missing in this scenario. Like a flash the answer came. It was a phoney self-effort kind of Christian life. This person was trying to prove that you are a Christian by grim determination. There is no joy in it. No wonder some feel the need to add a little so-called joy from the world. Such a person is an easy prey for the devil to get him back to his way of life.

What is lacking? It is the spontaneous outflow of the Holy Spirit in this Christian's life. The control of the Holy Spirit, the fullness of joy and love of God through the Holy Spirit are all lacking.

The Christian life is not a set of rules – do this, don't do that. Squeeze a little love out here, show a little kindness there. Ninety nine percent of the suggestions from the Bible Study class were positive, but it is the Holy Spirit who makes them alive. The Holy Spirit is able to do all these things through us if we will let Him. This is so different to the mechanical battle of trying to be a Christian through our own personal efforts.

In the book of Acts we see that the 3000 at Pentecost who repented and gave themselves to the Lord, started with the help of the Holy Spirit: "'What shall we do?' Then Peter said unto them, 'Repent (turn away from your old life of sin) and be baptised everyone of you in the name of Jesus Christ for the forgiveness of sins, and you will receive the gift of the Holy Spirit'" *(Acts 2:27, 38)* (KJ).

This is the Bible way. This is God's way. He knows that we won't get far without his Holy Spirit. Jesus made it quite clear when He commanded his disciples in *Acts 1:4* not to do anything, but to wait for the promise of the Father that they would be baptised with the Holy Spirit (v. 5). They tried to side-track Jesus with their minds still on earthly things by asking in verse 6: "Lord, wilt Thou at this time restore again the kingdom of Israel?" He had to bring them back to the most important point, namely: "But ye shall receive power after that the Holy Spirit is come upon you: and ye shall be witnesses unto Me both in Jerusalem, and in all Judaea, and in Samaria, and to the uttermost part of the earth" (v. 8).

Matthew 28:19–20 commands us as follows: "Go ye, therefore, and teach all nations, baptising them in the name of the Father, and of the Son, and of the Holy Spirit. Teaching them to observe things whatsoever I have commanded you." *Mark 16:17–18* tells us to use the authority of Christ to do five things:

1. To cast out demons;
2. To speak in new languages (the main purpose being prayer to God);
3. To have authority over serpents, and be kept safe;
4. To drink anything poisonous, and not be harmed;
5. To place their hands on the sick, and heal them.

Verse 20 continues: "And the disciples went everywhere preaching, and the Lord was with them, and confirmed what they said by the miracles that followed their messages." These were the last words of Jesus on earth, so every word was carefully selected to go into the canon of Scripture. We dare not disregard these words of our Saviour. No commands of Jesus can be accomplished without the Holy Spirit. The greatest need of the newly born Christian is the Holy Spirit's active work in his Life. If we don't allow the Spirit to work in our lives, our lives remain unfulfilled. The following scriptures tell us what we will be missing.

John 14:16 tells us one of his names is Comforter, the One who comes alongside to help in times of special need; *Ephesians 5:18* says that the Holy Spirit can fill our whole being so that our bodies are temples of the Holy Spirit; *Romans 5:5* says that He is the One who sheds abroad the love of God in our hearts; *Acts 1:8* says that without Him we have no power in witness. *John 16:13* tells us that we will have no guidance; *Galatians 5:22–23* that we won't have the fruit of the Spirit such as God's "love, joy, peace, patience, kindness, goodness, faithfulness, gentleness and self-control". We won't have the gifts of the Holy Spirit as found in *1 Corinthians 12:7–11*; and, finally, no miracles or results from our witness. *John 14:12* (LB) says that "Anyone believing in Me will do the same miracles." *Mark 16:17, 20* attests to similar things: "Those who believe in My name they will drive out demons, they will speak in new tongues, ... they will place hands on sick people and they will get well. The Lord worked with them and confirmed His Word by the signs that accompanied it."

What have we learned from our discussion? Take all the advice you can get from other Christians, but not before you have asked the Lord if it is good advice. He will give you a 'yes' or a 'no' in your innermost being. At the same time tell the Lord: "I know now, Lord, that I am not going to get anywhere without your Holy Spirit working in me. I surrender all my will to You so that You will control and guide my life. Keep me from being a "self-effort" Christian, and keep me depending on You."

The first Christians after Pentecost started off with the Holy Spirit. This is the clear picture in our minds. We are going to start off with Him, too. He is the One who is going to make Jesus real. He will enable us to hear the voice of the Saviour, and obey the Lord. He will make the Christian life vital and exciting! Why? Because He lives in us!

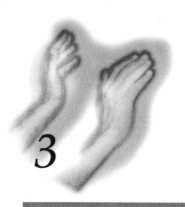

Introducing the Holy Spirit to you

3

Let us move into a mind-picture of what the Holy Spirit does as quickly as possible. What part He plays when we have come to Christ and know Him as our Saviour.

The promise of the Holy Spirit

The disciples were perturbed at the prospect of being parted from Jesus. Jesus explained to them that in order to fulfil the promise of the Holy Spirit's coming, He would need to return to heaven. This, in fact, would be an advantage to all believers, as He would live within them and empower their lives.

This is how Jesus put it to his disciples in *John 16:7*: "But I tell you the truth: It is for your good that I am going away. Unless I go away, the Counsellor will not come to you; but if I go, I will send Him to you." You see, in his bodily form, Jesus could only be in one place at a time. If He was in Jerusalem, He could not be in Galilee. The then known world was comparatively small. This problem would be far more serious today.

As usual, God had the perfect solution to the problem as is clear from *John 14:15–17 (LB)*: "If you love Me, obey Me, and I will ask the Father and He will give you another Comforter, and He will never leave you. He is the Holy Spirit, the Spirit who leads you into all truth ... He shall be in you." This word for "another" in the original is not another of a different kind to replace Jesus, but another of the same kind. The word used in the Greek is *allos*. It means another of the same kind, as used in *John 14:16* above.

Here is a delightful truth. The Holy Spirit is continuing the ministry of Jesus in an unlimited form. He is a true Person, just as Jesus and the Father are true Persons. The wonderful difference is that the Holy Spirit does not have a body, and therefore He can indwell the spirit of every believer. This is what we are taught in *John 15:25–27 (LB)*: "But I will send you the Comforter, the Holy Spirit, the source of all truth. He will come to you from the Father, and will tell you all about Me. And you also must tell everyone about Me."

Luke 24:49 repeats this: "And I will send the Holy Spirit upon you, just as My Father promised. Don't begin telling others yet ... wait until you are endued with His power from on high." So this is why the Holy Spirit had to come. He is Jesus' other self, and, whereas Jesus on earth was restricted in his movements, the Holy Spirit is not. From the time He came at Pentecost, the Holy Spirit lives in every believer in the Lord Jesus Christ, and may control him from within. That depends, of course, on the degree of one's surrender to Him. Don't misunderstand me. I am not saying the Holy Spirit is Jesus and Jesus the Holy Spirit. They are two separate persons in the Godhead, just as God the Father is a separate person. I am basically saying what *1 John 3:24* tells us, that Jesus lives in us through the Holy Spirit.

What a perfect arrangement! Only our heavenly Father could have planned such a relationship. He not only forgives, He empowers! Now let us examine what happens to people when they open their hearts to the Lord Jesus.

The Person and work of the Holy Spirit

Go back to the time you first began to realise that Jesus had a claim on your life, that He had bought you with his own precious blood. The Holy Spirit was there, though you did not realise it. He was the one bringing you to Christ.

In *John 16:8–9* (LB) we read of the task of the Holy Spirit: "And when He has come He will convince the world of its sin, and of the availability of God's goodness, and of deliverance from judgement. The world's sin in not believing in Me."

So it was He who worked in you to convince you that your own way would lead to destruction, and that you should turn away from it and take the path Jesus had mapped out for you. You began to hear Jesus knocking at your heart's door so that He might come in, as it is put in *Revelation 3:20*.

The Lord warns us against ignoring his knock in *Revelation 3:19*: "I continually discipline and punish (convict with instruction) every one I love; so I must punish you, unless you turn from your indifference and become enthusiastic about the things of God."

And so you did turn to the Lord. You heard Jesus knocking, and you were ashamed that you had left Him out for so long. You opened your heart to let

Jesus come into your life permanently. It was a little difficult to believe that He would actually come in to stay, but this assurance began to grow as you read other verses:

- *1 John 1:9:* "If we confess our sins, He is faithful and just to forgive us our sins, and to purify us from all unrighteousness."
- *1 John 1:7:* "The blood of Jesus, God's Son, purifies from every sin."
- *John 1:12:* "To all who received Him, to those that believed in His name, He gave the right to become children of God."

The knowledge that you had opened up your heart to Him, and that you had received Him, made it easier to believe that He was there. Then you turned the page and came on that breath-taking verse, *John 3:16* (KJ): "For God so loved the world that He gave His only begotten Son, that whosoever, (that included you) believeth in Him should not perish but have everlasting life."

Jesus has purchased eternal life for you. You have believed in Him, and His own life is in you by the Holy Spirit. You have everlasting life now and it cannot end, even in death. This is something to get enthusiastic about. Turning a few more pages, *John 6:37* (KJ) stands out like a neon light: "All that the Father giveth Me shall come to Me; and Him that cometh to Me I will in no way cast out." Even though you have felt yourself to be useless and unloved at times, God loved you and gave you to Jesus. Jesus says to you that you are much loved and you are precious to Him. The greatest assurance of all is that your place is reserved in heaven!" Almost every page in the New Testament contains further reassurance of God's love. In *John 10:10* we read that Jesus was aware of the devil's desire to take over God's throne. With his angels he had to be cast out of heaven. In *Luke 10:18* Jesus said "I saw Satan fall like lightning from heaven". The devil and his disciples, called evil spirits and demons, are now our adversaries. To get back to what Jesus said of the devil in John 10:10: "He has come to steal, to kill and destroy." We realise that we are not under the devil – the god of this world – anymore. The weakest Christian need not be afraid of him, but can command him to desist from his attacks on you. You have the power to do this in the Name of Jesus; you can bind Satan in every situation, always in the Name of Jesus. *Matthew 18:18* (KJ) tells us that "Whatsoever you shall bind on earth shall be bound in heaven." So tell the devil that you are not under his rule any longer, but that King Jesus rules your life. For as Jesus said in *John 10:10*: "I am come to give you life, and to give it more abundantly." That's why I like to be under King Jesus. I'm not taking death from the devil,

I am taking the more abundant life from Jesus.

When we get a little further in the same chapter, we read *John 10:27*, "My sheep hear My voice, and I know them, and they follow Me." Together we will listen to Jesus' voice and follow the Good Shepherd. Now listen to *John 10:28:* "And I give them eternal life; and they shall never perish, neither shall any man pluck them out of My hand." You talk about assurance that we belong to Jesus. This is *it!* We have eternal life in Jesus. No one can pluck us out of his hand.

If you should ever doubt your faith, Jesus added this specially for you: "My Father, Who gave them to Me, is greater than all, and no man is able to pluck them out of My Father's hand. I and the Father are one." *(John 10: 29–30)* This blesses me, and it blesses you! When you read this, feel strong in Jesus.

The Holy Spirit shows us all this in the Word, and his aim is to bring us the assurance of salvation. What is more, He is a living Person inside us. He is the same as Jesus in unlimited form, living in us as God's guarantee that we belong to Him.

The seal of the Holy Spirit is upon us

Already in the Old Testament we were promised that God would send his Spirit. *Ezekiel 36:25–27* tells us what this experience will be like: "Then it will be as though I had sprinkled clean water on you, for you will be clean – your filthiness will be washed away, your idol worship gone." Clean because of the blood of Christ! Free to reach out to Him. To worship Him: "And I will give you a new heart (that is, the spirit of our being). I will give you new and right desires, and put a new spirit within you. I will take out your stony heart of sin, and give you a new heart of love. And I will put my Spirit within you, so that you will obey my laws, and do whatever I command."

When do you receive a new spirit?

The moment you open your heart to Jesus. Let us turn to the New Testament now. *1 John 3:24* says: "And hereby we know that He abides in us by the Holy Spirit He has given us." *1 John 4:13* (LB) is even more explicit: "And He has put His own Holy Spirit into our hearts as proof to us that we are living in Him and He in us."

He doesn't live in our old, imperfect spirits, but in a new, recreated spirit which understands the things of God. So God's promise in Ezekiel becomes real. *2 Corinthians 5:17* tells us: "Therefore if any man be in Christ he is a new creation; old things are passed away, behold all things are become new." In *2 Corinthians 1:22* we read: "God who has sealed us and given us the guarantee of the Holy Spirit in our hearts (spirit)." These two verses together give us the picture of the Spirit in the innermost part of our bodies, recreated by the Holy Spirit. He lives within this new spirit, enabling us to hear the voice of the Lord in us. This is how the Good Shepherd speaks to his sheep. Two-way communication should take place all day long, and certainly takes place to give us the assurance that we belong to Him.

Romans 8:16 tells us that we are children of God because of the Spirit in us. If we do not have the Spirit, we are not his children (v. 9). Isn't this wonderful? Every Christian has the Holy Spirit living within. Dear child of God, a great intimacy with Jesus through the Holy Spirit is in store for you, but only if you are determined to obey the Master.

What is the reason for this sealing of the Holy Spirit? Did we suddenly deserve to have the Spirit living within? No. Jesus purchased this right for us by dying on the cross. We are "marked and sealed as belonging to Christ, by the Holy Spirit" *(Eph 1:13).*

The picture of the Holy Spirit living within is being confirmed and added to all the time. He is the guarantee of our future inheritance. As it is said in *Ephesians 1:14*: "His presence within us is God's guarantee that He will really give us all that He promised; and the Spirit's seal upon us means that God has already purchased us." Then we come to that powerful verse in *1 Corinthians 6:19* which emphasises: "Your body is the home of the Holy Spirit God gave you, and he lives within you. Your body does not belong to you." This promise is for all who believe, not only a select few: "For we were all baptised by one Spirit into one body, whether we be Jews or Gentiles, slave or free, and we were all given one Spirit to drink" *(1 Cor 12:13).*

No amount of self-effort could ever achieve a miracle like this. The Holy Spirit not only creates a new spirit within us; He does a special kind of Baptism. He baptises one into Christ's body. All Christians throughout the world, regardless of colour, now become part of the Body of Christ. When one lays hands on someone for healing, this hand is a part of Christ's Body, for God's power must work through a part of his Body.

How many of you believe you are part of Christ's Body? Now let me ask you a serious question. Are you going around, as Jesus did, doing good, healing the sick, casting out demons, helping to make disciples and making the power of God known on earth?

Thank God now for making you part of Christ's Body. Make this realisation part of your being. Now consult Him in everything, and receive your instructions from Him. Does this give you the faith to start moving ahead and begin doing what Jesus did?

The Living Bible leaves us in no doubt as to what is meant by *1 Corinthians 12:13*: "Each of us is a part of the one body of Christ. Some of you are Jews, some are Gentiles, some are slaves and some are free. But the Holy Spirit has fitted us all into one Body of Christ. We have been baptised into Christ's Body by the one Spirit, and have all been given that same Holy Spirit."

Christ in these days has to minister through his Body. Do you withhold yourself and reserve your body for yourself? Are you available to Him? He does not require our ability, but our availability! The whole message in these precious scriptures is summed up in another, *1 Peter 1:2* (LB): "Dear friends, God the Father chose you long ago and knew you would become His children. And the Holy Spirit has been at work in your hearts, cleansing you with the blood of Jesus Christ and enabling you to please Him."

Let us lay the foundation now. Believe that God does live in you through his Holy Spirit, that He is at work in your heart, cleansing you with the blood of Jesus. Oh, this makes us feel wonderful! I am sure we all want to please God, and the Holy Spirit at work in our hearts enables us to do just that. This is the scriptural picture. What you picture is what you believe!

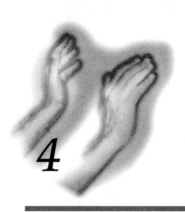

Learning to hear God's voice

4

Now that you have realised the importance of the Holy Spirit in your life and that you are not going to get very far without Him, let us try to understand who the Holy Spirit is, and what He does.

Our Lord Jesus could only be in one place at a time in his physical body on earth. He had been telling his disciples that He would have to return to his home in heaven. They were naturally disappointed. His words to them were: "If you love Me, obey Me, and I will ask the Father and He will give you another Comforter, and He will never leave you" *(John 14:15–16)*.

This word, another, as was explained previously, means another of the same kind. This makes me want to shout, Hallelujah! The Holy Spirit is the same kind as my Jesus, so Jesus has come back to live within me in His other self! This is even better, as He is no longer in a limited form as He was with a one-place-at-a-time body. He is now unlimited! We had better be careful from now on not to limit our Christ in the Holy Spirit to what we think He can or cannot do. From now on we shall find out what the Bible says He can do through us.

Now I am able to understand that the Holy Spirit is a Person, the same as Jesus. He can talk to us better than Jesus could to his disciples. Many of the things they heard they could not understand. They understood them, however, when the Holy Spirit came to dwell in them. What made the difference? The Holy Spirit recreates the spirit part of our being. God can now communicate, through our recreated or born-again spirits, to the mind, instead of trying to get through to a previously unregenerate spirit.

We have the mind of Christ!

In *1 Corinthians 2:16* we read: "We have the mind of Christ." If we believe this Scripture it is a great step towards getting our minds renewed. The mind of Christ is the mind of our new spiritual being that we have resident inside our body. As a person, you and I are each a child of God, we are a spirit, soul and body according to *1 Thessalonians 5:23*. This spirit is the spiritual being referred to above, complete with the mind of Christ. It is not the same as the natural mind contained in our brain cells. This mind which we call the soul is not reborn or recreated, nor is our body. We have a battle with our ordinary mind as it can be in conflict with the will of God. God tells us in *Romans 12:2*: "Do not conform any longer to the pattern of this world, but be transformed by the renewing of your mind. Then you will be able to test and approve what God's will is – His good, pleasing and perfect will."

From this Scripture we can readily see that the renewal of our mind will play a big part in being able to hear God's voice, and 'approve what God's will is'.

Why is this so?

Part of the answer can be found in the previous section. Our minds, unless renewed and adapted to the will of God, will block off and not receive what God is trying to tell us by means of our spirits. We should both believe that we have the mind of Christ and confess this truth. This is how we receive from God – by faith and by the confession from our mouths.

Let me explain: When we receive Jesus and become a child of God the above-mentioned principle is at work. Let me give you an example. One of the best and clearest salvation scriptures is *Romans 10:9*: "That if you confess with your mouth 'Jesus is Lord,' and believe in your heart that God raised Him from the dead, you will be saved." Do you see the principle at work here? We believe in our hearts and confess with our mouths what we believe. We have often thought that it is by faith alone that we receive from God, but it includes saying what we believe. If the word of God says that we have something in Christ, it does not follow that we receive it automatically. We believe this and declare that we have what we believe. This principle of how to receive from God always remains the same, for *Romans 10:10* declares: "For it is with your heart you believe and are justified, and it is with your mouth you confess and are saved." This works for our salvation and for everything else we receive from God. We believe we have the mind of Christ and confess this truth with our mouths.

It is thus essential for every Christian to picture clearly and exactly what happens when he gives his life to Christ. Without this clear picture, only confusion can result. Here is the clear, scriptural, mental image which builds an unshakeable faith presented to us in *Revelation 3:20*: "Look," (says Jesus) "I have been standing at the door and I am constantly knocking. If anyone hears Me calling him and opens the door, I will come in and enjoy fellowship with him and he with Me." Is this how you received Jesus? You could not bear to keep Him out any longer. You realised that Jesus died for you, died in your stead, because He loved you so much. So you opened the door of your heart to let Him in. Jesus said He would come in, so now He is living within you. You have his written word for it.

How does this happen?

The answer to this question lies in *1 John 3:24*: "And he that keepeth His commandments dwelleth in Him and He in him. And hereby we know that He (Jesus) abideth in us by the Holy Spirit whom He has given us." This is our assurance that Jesus has come to live within by the Holy Spirit. Isn't this wonderful! Since the time of Pentecost there is no waiting. The Holy Spirit comes in the moment we receive Jesus as Saviour.

What does the Holy Spirit do?

For the answer to this we go back to the Old Testament to look at some of God's most precious promises now fulfilled in the New Testament. *Ezekiel 36:26–27* says: "A new heart also will I give you and a new spirit will I put within you, and I will take away the stony heart out of your flesh, and I will give you a heart of flesh. And I will put my spirit within you and cause you to walk in My statutes, and ye shall keep my judgements, and do them."

These are among the most remarkable verses in the Old Testament. We humans are made of spirit, soul and body. The body is the vehicle; the soul is the personality which expresses itself through the five senses: touch, hearing, speech, smell and sight. In addition, the soul is made up of the mind, our total intellectual being, our will and emotions. Our mind must be renewed to think as God thinks. Our mind, will and emotions must be totally given over to God. If not, we live entirely on the level of the soul and provide only for the body and soul. Perhaps this is what most people do, so that the most important part, our spirit, is suppressed and kept under.

With the spiritual part of our being we are God-conscious, and we care for the things of God. The spirits of Adam and Eve were very much alive. They could talk to and receive answers from God. Immediately they had sinned, their spirits were cut off from God, their communication with Him broken down. Their physical death followed hundreds of years later. The point in explaining this is that we may understand that from that time onwards man's spirit has been dead toward God. Paul explains this in *1 Corinthians*

2:14 (KJ): "But the natural man receiveth not the things of the Spirit of God, for they are foolishness unto him; neither can he know them because they are spiritually discerned (understood)." Let us also read from the same passage in the Living Bible: "The man who hasn't the Holy Spirit can't understand and can't accept these thoughts from God, which the Holy Spirit teaches us. They sound foolish to him, because only those who have the Holy Spirit within them can understand what the Holy Spirit means. Others just can't take it in."

Now we can see that Jesus has restored to us all that we lost when Adam sinned. The ability to talk to and communicate with God has been bought back for us by our Lord Jesus. In fact, the Holy Spirit is our individual teacher. He understands what God wants to get through to us. This is how the Holy Spirit works.

The Holy Spirit renews us, and this is indicated in *2 Corinthians 5:17*: "Therefore if any man be in Christ, he is a new creature (new creation); the old things are passed away; behold, all things are become new." Now we see that *Ezekiel 36:26–27* which we read together has become a reality. The moment we receive Christ, the Holy Spirit comes in. He recreates the spirit which is our innermost being, and lives within this new human spirit. This is how the Holy Spirit can speak to us – through our spirits to our minds. Now we can tell the difference. When the devil tries to inject a thought from without, it is always a disturbing thought, and we can reject it in Jesus' name. The Holy Spirit, speaking from within our spirit, comes with a thought of truth and peace. This is how God communicates his will to us. He does indeed speak to us, and He speaks even to the youngest Christian. God is not able to get through to many Christians anymore, because they have let hardness creep in. Whenever God speaks, such Christians have already made up their minds not to obey Him, so God speaks less and less, and eventually they forget the sound of God's voice.

How soon may a Christian hear God's voice?

I shall never forget a true story our pastor, Edmund Roebert, told about a two-week old Christian. Pastor Ed, as we affectionately call him, at that time travelled over to Springs every Friday to preach at a home fellowship meeting while this Church was being established. Here is the story:

This man had just started to trust Jesus two weeks before, and he was now keen to bring some of his friends to the home meeting. On the way he felt thirsty, so, passing a café, he promptly popped in for a Coke. Inside he realised that he was walking in the wrong direction for a Coke, and turned in the right direction. At that instant God spoke to him, to his mind, in the first person. "I want you to stand just where you are," the Lord said. "But, Lord, the Cokes are over there," the man objected. Back came the instruction: "I want you to obey Me. Stand just where you are. You will understand in a moment." Do you see, here is a two-week-old Christian chatting to the Lord as to a friend, asking questions and getting instant replies. Most of us don't ask the Lord any questions, so we don't get any replies. There is no conversation with the Lord.

At that moment a very poor old woman walked in. She was wearing a very old, threadbare dress and cracked shoes. She was overheard asking the man behind the counter: "How much is the cheapest pack of mealie meal (corn meal) you've got?"

One who asks a question like that must be on his or her last few cents. Now God spoke again. "That money you have in your pocket. I want you to take it out and slip it into the old woman's hand without talking to her, and then walk straight out of the cafe." "But, Lord, that is the money I had reserved to buy those tackies tomorrow," he objected. "Don't worry about the tackies now. Do as I have told you." The instruction was so definite that the man obeyed. He folded the money into the old woman's hand and walked straight out of the cafe. He sat in his car for a few minutes and then saw the old woman come out with her pack of mealie meal. Her face was aglow with a beautiful smile which made our two-week-old Christian so happy that he had obeyed the Lord.

Now God spoke to him again. "Do you see that person walking toward the cafe? I want you to go and speak to her." "But what shall I say, Lord?" our friend replied. "I want you to obey Me, and I will give you the words to say," came the Lord's answer. I wish I knew the end of this story and what the Lord gave him to say, but I don't know.

When the Lord speaks to me, it is always in the first person. His words come from inside, not through my ears. It is God the Father speaking through the Holy Spirit, from my spirit to my mind. It is always definite, never begging, and is meant to be obeyed. This experience is not for the mature Christian only. I confess I had largely stopped hearing God's voice. I repented, confessed my sin, and God was gracious: He immediately started to speak to me again. The way to maintain this two-way communication is to apologise immediately to the Lord if you have disobeyed his voice. Ask Him what you should do to rectify the mistake, and obey his instructions.

Without this there is no real fulfilment in life. God reveals Himself to those who love and obey Him. Here are some scriptures which God has spoken so often to me from the book of John. The Lord repeats something when it is of great importance. I had read these words often in the King James Bible: "If you love Me, keep My commandments" *John 14:15*. As I recollect, I thought that this meant the Ten Commandments. I didn't realise that it meant the Lord's moment-by-moment instructions until I read the Living Bible.

Love and obedience are keys to hearing God's voice

1. *John 14:15:* "If you love Me, obey Me." These instructions are very important, for in the same theme Jesus mentions these points of loving and obeying nine times.

2. *John 14:21:* "The one who loves Me is the one who obeys Me ... and I will reveal Myself to him."

3. *John 14:23:* "I will only reveal Myself to those that love Me and obey Me." Do you want to be close to Jesus? This is the way!

4. *John 15:5:* "Apart from Me you can't do anything, ... But if you stay in Me and obey my commands, you may ask any request you like and it will be granted."

5. *John 15:10:* "When you obey Me, you are living in My *love.*"

6. *John 15:12:* "I demand that you love one another as much as I love you." We see that this is not optional; it is a command.

7. *John 15:14:* "You are My friends if you obey Me."

8. *John 15:17* (KJ) "These things I command, that ye love one another." Jesus' command enables us. How? By the power of the Holy Spirit He reveals Himself to those who love Him and are keen to obey Him.

Looking back

Jesus lives in us through the Holy Spirit. This is even better than when Jesus walked the earth with his disciples for three years. He taught and instructed them, yet after all that time they could not understand the spiritual lessons He taught. When Judas betrayed Him and courage was needed to stand by Jesus, they all fled. When pressed, Peter denied Him. After three years with Jesus, Peter could not preach, yet in possibly three hours after the Holy Spirit had entered into him and baptised (that is, immersed) him in his power, he preached one of the greatest sermons recorded in Scripture. In the same way, we need the Holy Spirit's power for service.

This is the importance of the Holy Spirit in our lives. He recreates the spiritual part of our being. It is a supernatural event, and in no way can we gradually develop this spiritual part of our being unless the Holy Spirit creates it and lives within. Then and only then, as we yield on all points of our lives, does He develop our spiritual attributes. This is the opposite of living in the realm of the soul, or mind.

Hebrews 4:12 (NIV) tells us the difference between soul and spirit: "The word of God is living and active. Sharper than any double-edged sword, it penetrates even to dividing soul and spirit ..." As reborn Christians, we begin to live more in the things of the spirit, and less in the soul side of life, in the realm of the mind. God says here in this Scripture that He wants our spirit divided from the soul. The separation between the two is essential if we are to hear what comes from God and distinguish what is just from our own thoughts or from the devil. The devil can influence us in the realm of the mind and the soul. Let us now look at the differences between soul and spirit:

Soul	Spirit
Feeling	Softness of heart and love to God and others
Hearing	Tuning in to the voice of God
Speaking	Witness to Christ and praying in the Spirit
Thinking	Spiritual intellect and knowing God
Seeing	Spiritual perception, discerning God's will

Christ has restored to us all that we lost when Adam sinned. We can actually get to know God's voice so clearly this way, that our lives become lives of loving and obeying God.

Just a word of caution from the Scriptures in respect of testing the spirits before we go on to other major aspects of the Holy Spirit's work. *1 John 4:1–4* says: "Dear friends, do not believe every spirit, but test the spirits to see whether they are from God, because many false prophets have gone out into the world. This is how you can recognise the Spirit of God: Every spirit that acknowledges that Jesus Christ has come in the flesh is from God, but every spirit that does not acknowledge Jesus, is not from God. This is the spirit of the antichrist, which you have heard is coming and even now is already in this world. You, dear children, are from God and have overcome them, because the one who is in you is greater than the one who is in the world."

Yes, the "Greater One" is living in you. You have a new "born-again" spirit in you. He is reliable. He never says a word against Jesus. In fact, one of the most important things in the Christian life, that of knowing inwardly that you are a Christian, is entrusted to the new spirit within. *Romans 8:16* tells us: "The Holy Spirit Himself testifies with our spirit that we are God's children." Our born-again spirit is indwelt by the Holy Spirit so the Holy Spirit communicates to our spirit by gentle feelings of peace and inward joy. It is a feeling of knowing inside. No rush, no forcing us into anything. Our will which we yielded to Jesus wants to co-operate. We find that Jesus' words in *John 10:27* became real: "My sheep listen to My voice; I know them, and they follow Me." You are his sheep.

To complete the picture we have been creating, I want you to see this. The Holy Spirit does not live in the human heart that pumps blood. He lives in the innermost being which is the real you. What is the "inner being" or "inner man" spoken of in *Ephesians 3:16*? This is your spirit, the real you. Your spirit looks just like you, except that he is perfect, without blemishes, he never grows old, and has no weight problems! In area he takes up the whole of your body. Where does the Holy Spirit live? In your re-created spirit, so the whole of your body becomes the temple of the Holy Spirit.

Why explain this? So that we can picture who we really are. I am a spirit. I possess a soul, that is the mind the emotions and the will, and I live in my body. Now it is easy to see that the Holy Spirit takes up residence in the whole of my body as his temple. *1 Corinthians 6:19* affirms this: "Do you not know that your body is a temple of the Holy Spirit, who is in you, whom you have received from God? You are not your own; you are bought with a price. Therefore honour God with your body."

How will you be sure that you are hearing God's voice?

If you long to hear God's voice clearly, you must be able to discern the Holy Spirit controlling your mind, as God speaks in your thought patterns, not an audible voice as *Romans 8:6* tells us: "The mind of sinful man is death, but the mind controlled by the Holy Spirit is life and peace."

I want my mind controlled by the Holy Spirit, don't you? Then He can communicate to you more easily, can't He?

What do we need to do? We need to constantly yield our brains to his control. If we don't, we will be mind-led instead of being led by the Holy Spirit. *Romans 8:14* tells us that if we are not led by the Spirit of God, we are not his children. I want to come back to *Romans 8:16* which we looked at a moment ago as I think I did not emphasise a vital point enough. It says, "The Spirit Himself testifies with our spirit that we are God's children." This is the most important thing we know, it is the assurance of our salvation. We call this 'the inward witness' and it is a great spiritual breakthrough to know how God speaks to us. How do we actually experience the 'Holy Spirit testifying with our spirit'? Couldn't we analyse it by saying that we have a deep knowing inside that we are children of God?

Yes, I think we can. The moment you receive Jesus as our Saviour you begin to have this knowing on the inside, which we call an inward witness. It is a comfortable feeling inside, a feeling of assurance and joy. In less spiritual, more down-to-earth terms we might say, a 'gut feeling' or an intuition. This is the Holy Spirit speaking to our inward selves.

Paul said in *Romans 9:1*: "I speak the truth in Christ, I am not lying, my conscience confirms it in the Holy Spirit." This was God speaking to him. We should never go against our conscience, we should flow with it. In the New Testament we are not led by prophets. In the Old Testament the ordinary person did not have the help of the Holy Spirit but the prophet did, so that people could get guidance from the prophet. In our day, every child of God is indwelt by the Holy Spirit, so that the sons of God are led by the Spirit of God. We should settle for nothing less! We can be filled "with the knowledge of His will through all spiritual wisdom and understanding *(Col 1:9)*. We don't get this from our brains; this spiritual wisdom comes from the Holy Spirit through our born-again spirits.

The New Testament Christian should never put out a fleece. This attempt to seek guidance is in the physical and mental realm in which the devil operates. Put out a fleece and you will be fleeced! The children of God are led by an inward witness from the Spirit of God. Let us confess every day that, "As a child of God I am led by the Spirit of God." *2 Corinthians 5:7* tells us, "We live by faith not by sight."

My pastor Ed, now gone to be with the Lord, had tremendous wisdom in knowing what to do in leading one of the largest churches in Africa. He told me he never made a move without hearing from, and then obeying, what the Holy Spirit communicated to him through his spirit and then to his mind. This came with assurance from within. Paul said in *Acts 23:1* (KJ): "I have lived in all good conscience before God until this day." I know pastor Ed could say the same.

1 John 5:10 (KJ) tells us, "He that believeth on the Son of God hath the witness in himself." This is similar to *Romans 8:16* above and refers to the same experience, and God is reassuring us that we belong to Him. What we need to find out is if there are various ways in which this inward witness can come to us.

How does the inward witness come to us?

Let us look at a few pointers in this regard:

1. How did God speak to the 'two week old Christian'? Well, the way he described it, it was in words directly to him and not audible to others; one could say audible to him, only to the inner ear. While I am writing words are coming to me all the time. My natural mind does not have the ability to understand how all these spiritual things work. Let us go back to *Colossians 1:9*: "To fill you with the knowledge of His will through all spiritual wisdom and understanding." How does this come to us? God communicates through his Spirit to the spiritual intellects of our spirits and this is transferred to our brains for our understanding. This is God speaking to us in our natural thought patterns.

We can get thoughts from three sources: Our own thoughts, the devil can inject thoughts and God can put thoughts into our minds. How will we know the difference? We can and should discuss things with God. Ask Him if it is Him speaking and repeat the thought to Him. If it is from God you will have an immediate and repeated feeling of peace from inside, what can be described as a witness from within. The more you think about it, the better you will feel about it. If the thought is from the devil, you will feel a little uneasy, a little scratchy, about it. This is a check from your spirit. Never act on that, but resist the devil in Jesus' name.

2. God speaks to our mind in pictures which people might call a vision. It can be a moving or a still picture. The pictures could come in our dreams, but this must certainly be checked out with the Lord, as I have said above.

3. When you need to hear from God, ask Him a direct question. Ask in faith, expecting an immediate answer. Expect by faith that the next thoughts, or pictures that pop into your mind will be God communicating to you. This always needs to be confirmed with God in the way indicated above. The gifts of the Spirit, like a word of knowledge or word of wisdom, will work this way too. If you are able to pray in tongues this is a big help in hearing from God. In tongues you speak to God, then ask God to speak back to you. He will speak back to you in your normal thought pattern. This is called interpretation of tongues. I will talk about this in greater detail when we discuss the gifts of the Spirit.

4. God will never tell you to do anything contrary to his Word. If you don't know the Bible well ask a friend who might know, or use a concordance to check. Remember God's will is never in conflict with his Word.

5. God can speak in other ways, but mostly a Christian will go through an entire life-time without having a spectacular vision such as a visitation by an angel. Don't look for the spectacular.

6. One of the most common ways for God to speak to you is that while reading the Bible He will quicken a Scripture or part of a verse to you and you will have a knowing inside that God is communicating to you. You also have to confirm this with the Lord, as the devil can use God's Word – like he did with Eve.

7. Remember God is interested in everything you are interested in. If you have to make a business deal, God is interested in that and you need his guidance. Ask him questions about it. If you need work in your business, God can dispatch angels to help you. Why not ask for his help? He can help you in your work and play, in the friends you need and in the choice of a partner. There is no limit to God's interests in your life. God says in *Psalm 32:8*: "I will instruct you and teach you in the way you should go; I will counsel you and watch over you." God is intensely interested in you. So, in line with *Proverbs 3:6–8*, "Trust in the Lord with all your heart and lean not to your own understanding; in all your ways acknowledge Him, and He will make your paths straight. Do not be wise in your own eyes; fear the Lord and shun evil. This will bring health to your body."

Do you understand how inner witness can come to you? Now go for it!

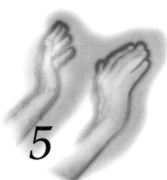

Three major aspects of the Holy Spirit's work

5

In the early Seventies, after I had been baptised with the Holy Spirit, the Lord laid it heavily upon my heart to make a thorough study of the Holy Spirit and his working in our lives.

The phrase "baptised with the Holy Spirit", means "immersed with his power". The Scriptures use the word "baptised" so no apology is necessary. If it is preferred, the phrase "Endued (clothed) with power from on high" (Luke 24:49) may be used instead. If you are abiding in Christ you have Him all around you, don't you? How does He envelop you? By the Holy Spirit. Don't let terms and words rob you of the experience of his power.

I felt that the only way to see the doctrine of the Holy Spirit clearly would be to put together all the Scriptures on the Holy Spirit. In this way, one could read all these verses like a book on the Holy Spirit, and they would not be man's opinion, but God's Word. From this I hoped a clear picture would emerge. This enquiry took two and a half years, when I had thought it would take no more than two months. God would wake me up at 3:00 or 4:00 in the morning, and I would find it impossible to stay in bed any longer. When God did this, I never felt tired. His Divine energy would flow through me.

The study, in which four Bibles were used, fell under seven natural headings. Under each heading, I went through the Scriptures from Matthew to Revelation. The Scriptures were cut out and glued in columns onto loose-leaf pages, just like those in the Bible. I know there is an easier way to do this now on a computer, but in those days computers for personal use were not even thought of! These are the subject headings:

	No. of pages
1. How and why the Holy Spirit came	1
2. The Holy Spirit's person and work	6
3. How the Holy Spirit is received	4

→

4. How to be filled with the Holy Spirit	32
5. How to be baptised with the Holy Spirit	25
6. The baptism into the Body of Christ by the Spirit	2
7. The result: Working in the power of the Holy Spirit	19
Total	**89 pages**

When one reads the Bible, a Scripture here and there registers in the mind. It may speak about the Holy Spirit. Sure enough, a picture of what the Holy Spirit does is painted in the mind. Could one imagine that these Scriptures would total 89 pages? I know I didn't! If the number of pages God wrote on the subject is an indication of its importance, then it is easy to see that to Him it is tremendously important that we be filled and baptised with the Holy Spirit. It might come as a surprise that these three headings below appear as separate entities of one whole:

1. How the Holy Spirit is received as God's Gift.
2. How to be filled with the Holy Spirit and controlled by Him.
3. How to be baptised with the Holy Spirit and be used by Him.

God wants his children to have this threefold experience as one whole, as at Pentecost. As we look at his Church today, this is not the case. Many have only Part 1. Others have Parts 1 and 2 or Parts 1 and 3. Christians who have a combination of all three are relatively few in number. This position is changing rapidly, as God is making Christians keenly aware, in this glorious end time, of his will in respect of the Holy Spirit. Here follows an enlarged picture of these three points:

How the Holy Spirit is received as God's gift

The reception of the Holy Spirit happens at conversion. It is really impossible to be a Christian and not have the Holy Spirit coming in to live in the Christian's innermost being. This was promised in the Old Testament and is now a reality for all Christians. The promise is from *Ezekiel 36:26–27*, as we have seen before: "I will give you a new heart and put a new spirit in you; I will remove from you your heart of stone and give you a heart of flesh. And I will put my spirit in you and move you to follow my decrees and be careful to obey My commands."

In fact, the Holy Spirit recreates the spirit part of the Christian and lives within every believer, as we see in the following scriptures:

2 Corinthians 5:17: "Therefore, if anyone is in Christ, he is a new creation; the old has gone, the new has come!"

2 Corinthians 1:22: "God has anointed us, set His seal of ownership on us, and put His Spirit in our hearts as a deposit, guaranteeing what is to come." (As for example, a greater filling and a greater relationship in power for service).

1 Corinthians 3:16: "Don't you know that you yourselves are God's temple and that God's Spirit lives in you?"

1 Corinthians 6:19–20: "Your body is a temple for the Holy Spirit, who is in you, whom you have received from God. You are not your own; You were bought at a price (through His Son). Therefore honour God with your body." The Holy Spirit lives in the human spirit, and makes us God-conscious, and witnesses that we are his children.

Romans 8:16: "The Spirit Himself testifies with our spirit that we are God's children." This Christian begins to live not as a mind-dominated or sinful person, but in the Spirit.

1 Corinthians 2:14 (KJ): "The natural man (or the person controlled merely by his sinful mind) receiveth not the things of the Spirit of God: for they are foolishness to him, neither can he know them, because they are spiritually discerned." We can readily see that a person like this lives in the five senses only. A Christian should show a willingness to be taught by the Holy Spirit.

Christ lives in every Christian. How? Through the Holy Spirit. *John 3:24* tells us this: "He abides in us by the Holy Spirit he has given us." In all these scriptures we see the gift of the Holy Spirit.

It seems to me that by far the greater majority of Christians throughout the world are in this category. I was there from my conversion in 1937 to 1947, when I experienced the in-filling of the Holy Spirit. There is a definite difference between the gift and the filling of the Holy Spirit. Through reading books and God's Word, I had a great longing to be filled with the Holy Spirit. I wondered how this could happen. I finally realised that if I was to be filled with the Holy Spirit, I could not earn this privilege. It had to be like any experience we might receive from God – by faith. This I had confirmed to me in *Galatians 3:2, 5, 14*, regardless of how I felt. Read the following quotation from the Scriptures:

"Did you receive the Spirit by observing the law, or by believing what you heard? ... Does God give you His Spirit and work miracles among you because you observe the law, or because you believe what you heard? ... He redeemed us in order that the blessing given to Abraham might come to the

Gentiles through Christ Jesus, so that by faith we might receive the promise of the Spirit."

As a young farmer, I was studying Dr R.A. Torrey's book *What the Bible teaches*, together with my neighbours. Several times I tried to lead them to the Lord, but failed. Now I had trusted the Lord for the filling of the Holy Spirit. My immediate neighbour walked home with me part of the way. On one particular evening, I suggested again that he give himself to Christ. This time there was no opposition. We both knelt in the dust of the road and he prayed, asking the Lord to forgive his sins and to come and live within him. I had led my first soul to the Lord. I was filled with joy. The witness of the Father was saying to me, "You see, you trusted me to fill you, and this has happened. That is why it was easy to win your neighbour to the Lord." I told my mother. She trusted the Lord for the filling of the Holy Spirit. This became a reality to her, too, and she led a prisoner, condemned for murder, to the Lord.

We had trusted the Lord previously as Saviour and had the joy of having our sins forgiven. The Holy Spirit was living within the recreated human spirit, but I for one did not know that one could be filled with the Holy Spirit. Looking back now, I know that *Romans 8:10–11, 16* was real to me: "But if Christ is in you ... He will also give life to your mortal body through His Spirit, who lives within you." (This refers to God's gift.) "The Holy Spirit Himself witnesses with our spirit that we are God's children." This to me was the gift of the Holy Spirit. I could not be a Christian without the Holy Spirit living within me.

To define clearly again what is meant by the term *gift* of the Holy Spirit: With the *gift* one possesses the Holy Spirit, but with the *filling*, He possesses us. This is a continuing process and He should possess us more and more fully as we yield and obey (Acts 5:32) to each step He shows us. This is the same as the *sealing* with the Holy Spirit, as we read in *Ephesians 4:30*: "And do not grieve the Holy Spirit of God, by whom you were sealed for the day of redemption." When Peter used the term "gift" in his sermon *Acts 2:38*, it was in answer to the question the people had asked: "Brothers, what shall we do?" Peter replied, "Repent and be baptised, every one of you, in the name of Jesus Christ the Messiah so that your sins may be forgiven. And you will receive the gift of the Holy Spirit." We know that the Holy Spirit is the author of the Bible. The Holy Spirit here prevented Peter from using the word "baptism" in this context, but chose instead the term "gift". God knew that three thousand would be converted to the Messiah that day and they all received God's "gift", the Holy Spirit, Who was to live within their newly recreated human spirits. It is just possible that some also received the baptism of the Holy Spirit at the same time. Scripture is silent on that point. The next verse, 42, says that these three thousand believers, "devoted themselves to the apostles' teaching and to the fellowship, to the breaking of bread and to prayer." Since they continued with the Lord, the great likelihood is that most, and I hope all, went on to the filling and baptism with the Holy Spirit.

All Christians are baptised into the body of Christ. They become part of the world-wide body of the Messiah. This transcends all denominations, and is the work of the Holy Spirit. *1 Corinthians 12:13* reads: "For we were all baptised by one Spirit into one body – whether Jews or Greeks, slave or free, and we have all been offered to drink into one Spirit." The last part is my own translation, which I feel is more accurate since this part refers to the baptism with the Holy Spirit, done by Jesus. Thayer's *Greek Lexicon*, in explaining the Greek word *Potidzo*, notes that it means "to offer one something to drink". In this context, the same word is used in *Matthew 10:42* and *Romans 12:20*.

This baptism by Jesus is not forced on you. You are not "made" to have it, as the King James version suggests. It is an "offer". Jesus will do this for you if you ask Him for it. *Luke 3:16* says: "He will baptise you with the Holy Spirit." Note again, this baptism is done by Jesus. The baptism into the body of Christ is by the Holy Spirit.

There is a price to pay – the price of dedication and obedience. The 120 at Pentecost paid this price. They therefore received the "threefold" experience of the Holy Spirit, explained in this chapter, as a single experience and not as three separate experiences.

This does happen today, and it should, when a newly-born Christian is being discipled and counselled about these three aspects of the Holy Spirit. We are not doing God a favour by inviting Christ to live within. It is our obligation to open wide the door of our lives for Christ, through the Holy Spirit in his all-enveloping power.

How to be filled with the Holy Spirit

It was ten years later, at the age of 25, that I experienced the filling of the Holy Spirit. This does not refer to the baptism of the Holy Spirit followed by the manifestation of the gifts. It means the inward controlling power of the Holy Spirit to live a changed life, in keeping with the life of Christ manifested in his children.

This experience of being filled with the Spirit followed a time during which God showed me that I had taken something that did not belong to me. It was a painful experience, but God convicted me, and I knew I had to write a letter when returning the article, and also send cash as compensation, explaining why. It was a time of confessing all known sin, getting my heart cleansed. The sort of picture I had in my mind was that the Holy Spirit had been living in me previously, but I had limited Him in my life. I had confined Him to a small area. I hadn't been so sensitive to sin. Now I was very eager to get rid of anything that might grieve the Holy Spirit. Everything He told me to get rid of, I would confess and have it washed away with the precious blood of Christ. The clear picture of the spiritual experience I was having was that in the centre my heart was a clean, bright area. This was where the Holy Spirit lived. All round were black blotches like ink spots. As I confessed these, the black spots were washed away by the wonderful cleansing power of Jesus' blood. The place where He could live was rapidly being enlarged since the soulish area was being diminished.

The Holy Spirit was known to me now as a Person. I did not want to grieve Him in any way. Everything He spoke to me about, I was eager to correct. I wanted above all things for Him to fill me. It was as though He had been living in the lounge. Now I was eagerly opening the other rooms to Him. Then it came to some cupboards. I was hoping He would not go into detail about the little things. The big issues I could see should be opened up to Him; the small things, things I read in the newspaper or magazines, or the kind of music I filled my mind with surely were not his concern. I only wanted to obey Him when it suited me, and not all the time. These did not relate to a great God. I silently prayed: "Pass over these small things, Lord. Let us restrict your scrutiny to the larger rooms. Your interest should stop there." I did not want to open the smaller cupboards. Finally, I gave the Holy Spirit the keys to open up everything in my life. This was my complete surrender to his control.

Now the Holy Spirit filled me. I took the plunge by faith, the same as when I received Christ as Saviour. Now the experience was sweet. Gone was the battle of trying to keep the Holy Spirit out of certain areas of my life. I had a peace and calmness, a victory over anger, temper and many other sins in my life. It was then that I led my neighbour to the Lord. I had a new zeal to lead the Africans on the farm to the Lord. I had always worked with them and knew their language well. Now we started the day by praying together. In a short while I led everyone in my African Sunday school class to the Lord. What a joy I had in my spirit. When the Holy Spirit put his finger on a new area in my life, previously unwrapped, I was able to surrender easily to his control.

Looking back, I can see now I was enjoying the *fruit of the spirit*, as listed in *Galatians 5:22–23*: "Love, Joy, Peace, Patience, Kindness, Goodness, Faithfulness, Gentleness and Self-control."

The difference between the Gift of the Holy Spirit and the Filling became very plain. With the Gift, He came in to live within, but I tried to control Him. Now I had surrendered to Him, and He was controlling me! At first I possessed the Holy Spirit, now He was possessing me.

Being controlled by the Holy Spirit is the official theme of the Great Keswick Convention in England, a theme widely held by Baptists all over the world and also propagated by the non-charismatic Christian world. From my study of the scriptures, I had compiled 30 large Bible pages on the subject, so this is scriptural truth. It leads to a Christian living a holy, sanctified life, a life of dedication and stability. This is the *Pimplemi* filling which Peter had in *Acts 4:8* and John the Baptist in *Luke 1:15*: "He will be filled with the Holy Spirit even from before his birth." Not a once-for-all filling, but an oft-repeated one.

It is not a life of self-effort. *The Holy Spirit* brings one into a victorious and holy Christian life, a life experiencing the *fruit* of the spirit quoted above. Here we are not referring to the Holy Spirit's power for service which will be referred to later. This is the message of *Ephesians* all the way through, from *Ephesians 3:16 to 6:10*, with the crowning verse, 5:18 in the middle: "Be filled with the Holy Spirit." *Ephesians 3:16* says: "I pray that out of His glorious riches He may strengthen you with power through His Spirit in your inner being".

From here on, the context is: "How a beautiful Christian life can be lived with victory over sin." This is the kind of life Jesus lived. The only difference was that his life was perfect, without sin, as He had the continuous, complete *Pleres*-type of filling spoken of in *Luke 4:1*. This filling of the Holy Spirit began when the Holy Spirit planted the seed in Mary's womb. It was in the power of the Holy Spirit that Jesus, all through his childhood years, and right on up to the age of 30, lived this beautiful, perfect, sinless life. He denied that He was good in his own right. The other difference between us and Jesus is that He did not have the old sinful nature within. He was 100 % human in body, but also 100 % God at the same time.

In order to become like Jesus, we are commanded in *Ephesians 4:22–23* (New Trans.) to "Put off concerning the former way of life the old nature and be renewed in the spirit of your mind. And that you put on the new nature, which in the likeness of God has been created in righteousness and holiness of the truth."

Every verse we look at in these chapters has as its goal the cleansing of the Christian life. Take any verses at random, such as *Ephesians 4:31–32:* "Get rid of all bitterness, rage, anger, brawling and slander, along with every form of malice. Be kind and compassionate to one another, forgiving each other, just as in Christ, God forgave you."

If we cling to the former things in the above scripture, we hold on to darkness. *Ephesians 5:8* says: "For you were once darkness, but now you are light in the Lord. Live as children of light." Light here is not ordinary light; it is the Light personified in the Holy Spirit. In this regard, compare *Ephesians 5:9* "The fruit of the *light* (the Spirit) consists in all goodness, righteousness and truth."

Here is a basis for picturing the Holy Spirit. He is *light.* Jesus we can picture easily, as He has a body like ours. We can easily picture the Father, as Jesus said: "Philip, he that hath seen Me hath seen the Father" *(John 14:9).* So the Father is just like Jesus, only so majestic that we could not look on Him with our present bodies and live *(Exod 33:18–21).*

Where does the Holy Spirit fill us?

He lives within our recreated spirit, so He fills our spirits in what Jesus called "the innermost part of our being". We can picture Him there flooding us with His light, taking full charge and control from the heart. This is in contrast to our controlling everything from the mind, and not first listening to what the Holy Spirit is saying. This is the practical outworking of the Holy Spirit in his fullness. He is given charge of spirit, soul and body.

The filling by the Holy Spirit works out in practically every area of our lives. What the Word says in *Ephesians 5:18* is that we won't manage this new way of living by our own self-effort. The *Living Bible* says, "Be filled instead with the Holy Spirit and be controlled by Him." I like this, don't you?

Jesus lived his life without sinning, in the power of the Holy Spirit. We won't get far if we try anything less! God showed me that the filling of the Holy Spirit is maintained by an attitude of constant submission, repentance and faith toward Him, by facing temptation strongly in the powerful name of Jesus, and by an attitude of praise.

How to be baptised with the Holy Spirit

For 25 years I had been filled with the Holy Spirit. Now the charismatic renewal came flooding into our church, and it seems that hardly a church anywhere is left out. Some leaders have tried to stamp it out, even by ruthlessly removing dear fellow Christians from their churches. This is not the fruit of love.

Leaders, do not call your own experience of the filling with the Holy Spirit in question by acting without love. *Ephesians 4:2* says: "Be completely humble and gentle; be patient, bearing with one another in love, and make every effort to keep the unity of the Spirit through the bond of peace."

In 1972 our Pastor, Edmund Roebert, took a series of Bible Studies on the Baptism with the Holy Spirit and the manifestation of his gifts. At the conclusion of the thirteenth lecture, my wife, Ivy, and I both said, "This experience is for us". Ed prayed for us with the laying on of hands. We received the Baptism with the Holy Spirit by faith, and commenced at first with difficulty to use the gift Jesus Himself had promised. We read in *Mark 16:17*: "And these signs will accompany those who believe; in My Name ... they will speak in new tongues." I don't think I spoke more than three words that first evening.

Over a period of four months, a greater fluency came in this prayer language, especially while I was driving to work alone. Now, depending on what I am doing, this prayer language has flowed through me for up to 18 hours in one day, while on a long trip by car. The Holy Spirit's energising flow is effortless and keeps one from getting tired. God always gets the glory for something the Holy Spirit does through us as his children.

What are the qualifications for the baptism in the Holy Spirit?

1. These qualifications are the same as for the filling. All we ever receive from God is by faith. We cannot deserve or earn anything that God can give. The pattern when we received Jesus Christ as Saviour is the same as for the baptism. We received Him into our hearts by faith. The basis of our faith is always God's Word.

God might have spoken to us through his Word, for example *Revelation 3:20:* "Behold, I stand at the door and knock. If anyone will hear My voice and open the door I will come in." So you opened your heart to Jesus, and He came in. How did you know? You believed his Word! This happened to me. This is the very Scripture God used to bring me to Jesus. We can look at the following passage of scripture which makes any experience with the Holy Spirit clear:

Galatians 3:2: "I would like to learn just one thing from you: Did you receive the (Holy) Spirit by observing the law or by believing what you heard?" Verse 3 is also appropriate: "Are you so foolish? After beginning in the Spirit, are you now trying to attain your goal by human effort?" And verse 5: "Does God give you His (Holy) Spirit, and work miracles among you, because you observe the Law or because you believe what you heard?"

To reinforce this teaching from God's Word, v. 14 says: "He redeemed us ... so that by faith we might receive the promise of the Holy Spirit" and, may I add, of his working in our lives in his many aspects.

2. A deep, yielding spirit is required, but, as we have seen above, not through self-effort. Coupled with the surrender should be a quick and deep repentance, for we cannot cling to anything which might hinder the Holy Spirit. It is very easy to pride yourself on the impeccable life you feel you are now living. Such pride, unless repented, will hinder the baptism in the Holy Spirit.

The finest way to get rid of the unwanted rubbish in one's life is to have it burnt away, one of the results of the "Baptism with the Holy Spirit and Fire" *(Luke 3:16)*. That is what fire is for, for we are so bound by traditions, biases and rebellion against the working of the Holy Spirit. Shadrach, Meshach and Abednego had their bonds burnt away very quickly in Nebuchadnezzar's fiery furnace! *(Dan 3:16–18)*. Allow the Holy Spirit to burn all your bonds away without delay so that you are ready for his baptism.

3. Who baptises with the Holy Spirit? I am so glad that Jesus does this. He baptises with the Holy Spirit. We all have a special confidence if Jesus does the work, don't we? John the Baptist said in *Luke 3:16*: "He (Jesus) shall baptise you with the Holy Spirit and Fire."

What we read in *Luke 11:11–13* is confirmed in *Matthew 7:11*. From these scriptures we have the assurance that we will only get what we ask. *Luke 11:11:* "Which of you Fathers, if your son asks for bread, will give him a stone; or if he asks for a fish, will give him a snake instead? Or if he asks for an egg, will give him a scorpion? If you then, though you are evil, know how to give good gifts to your children, how much more will your Father in heaven give the Holy Spirit to those who ask Him?"

This is God's assurance that we will get what we ask for. Ask for bread and you will get bread. Ask for the baptism with the Holy Spirit, and you will receive the baptism. Ask for a prayer language and you will be given a prayer language. *Matthew 7:11* refers to gifts. People often have an apprehension that they may not get what they ask for. They wonder if perhaps they may get something from the devil. We can all rest assured that we will get what we ask for. These scriptures are God's guarantee that this will be so. Go right ahead and ask!

4. Is the baptism with the Holy Spirit essential? As we have already explained, Jesus had been filled with the Holy Spirit for 30 years. When He launched into his public miracle-working ministry with all the gifts working through Him, his was a new experience of the Holy Spirit. The account of Jesus being baptised or immersed in water and being baptised with the Holy Spirit is in all four Gospels (Matt 3:16; Mark 1:11; Luke 3:22 and John 1:32). In Luke 3:22, we are told what happened in these words: "The Holy Spirit descended upon Him in bodily form like a dove." John 1:32 puts it this way: "Then John gave this testimony: 'I saw the Spirit come down from heaven as a dove and remain on Him.'"

Jesus did not have the gifts of the Holy Spirit manifested through Him up to that time. He had not healed any sickness nor performed any miracles up to this point in his ministry. If this immersion and power operation of the Holy Spirit was so necessary for Jesus, how much more necessary it is for us.

5. Is the baptism with the Holy Spirit a command? Jesus thought the baptism was so essential for his followers that He commanded it, for He Himself did nothing in his ministry apart from the Holy Spirit's baptism of power.

Luke 24:45–49 (KJ) sets out his instructions to his disciples: "Then opened He their understanding that they might understand the Scriptures, and said unto them, Thus it is written and thus it behoved Christ to suffer and to rise from the dead the third day, and that repentance and remission of sins (forgiveness) should be preached in his Name among all nations beginning at Jerusalem. And ye are witnesses of these things, and behold I send the promise of My Father upon you, but tarry ye in the city of Jerusalem, until ye be endued with power from on high."

If we come with humility before the Lord without a bias or any preconceived ideas, we shall receive an imparted understanding of the Scriptures regarding the baptism of the Holy Spirit.

First comes repentance. This is a definite act when we decide to turn from all sin. There is another sense in which from then on we must continuously turn away from all sin and pride in every situation saying, "No, I choose God's way." That is why praise from the heart is such a valuable weapon. You can't praise God without reaching out to Him. That is why you see people's hands going up automatically as an act of worship. Praise is one of the ways to remain continuously repentant.

Secondly, there is *forgiveness or remission* of every sin. *Remission* means a complete and total release from a sentence we were found guilty of. There is no doubt we were guilty, but Jesus our Lord took the punishment of our sins upon Himself. We must accept his forgiveness. Enjoy the fact of being forgiven; it's a total remission. God can't even remember any bad thing you did. Don't you accept guilt from the devil when he tries to remind you!

Because you have been forgiven, you can now forgive others freely, too. Don't make the mistake of withholding forgiveness from anyone. Always ask forgiveness and give forgiveness very quickly. To refuse is to open one's self to successive calamities from Satan. Why? Because an opening is made in your armour for him to attack through. Read *Matthew 18:21–35*. The unforgiving servant was turned over to the "tormentors". Verse 35 says: "This is how My Heavenly Father will treat each of you unless you forgive your brother from your heart." These two things, forgiveness and repentance, are basic if we want to receive the baptism with the Holy Spirit. Any hesitation becomes a hindrance.

You do not need to wait or "tarry" any longer than it takes you to repent, receive and give forgiveness. The Holy Spirit has been waiting since Pentecost to take possession of you and baptise you with his mighty power. The Scripture in *Luke 24:49*, which we read together, is so definite as to be a command. *Acts 1:4–5* tells us it was a command: "He gave them this command: 'Wait for the *gift* my Father promised, which you have heard me speak about. For John baptised in water, but in a few days you will be baptised with the Holy Spirit.'"

Clearly this experience of the Holy Spirit is not an optional extra to the Christian life. Jesus commanded us as his followers to be baptised with the Holy Spirit. It is our duty to obey Him in everything He says in his Word.

6. What is the baptism with the Holy Spirit? This is the operative power of the Holy Spirit to enable God's children to witness for their Saviour without fear. It is the operative power of the Holy Spirit to enable God's children to stand up against their adversary, the devil, and command him in Jesus' name to flee. From now on, you don't get pushed around by the devil. You realise who you are – no less than a blood-bought child of the Almighty God, with Jesus as your Elder Brother. You just have to use his powerful name and the devil cringes, and can't get away fast enough. By first submitting to God, you can resist the devil in Jesus' name. Then you will see him fleeing away (*Jas 4:7*).

This is the *"upon"* relationship of the Holy Spirit where He literally comes upon you, baptising you with Himself. He immerses you, envelops you in his Power, so that at last He can begin to use you, instead of you trying to use Him. *Acts 1:8* sums it up: "But you will receive power when the Holy Spirit *comes on you*; and you shall be my witnesses." Unless we make a mockery of the verbal inspiration of the Bible, we have to believe what the Word says here. We know we have the inheritance at conversion. We must claim the inheritance and experience the power. This is the "upon" relationship that Jesus had when the Holy Spirit *came upon Him* and remained on Him *(John 1:32)*.

Remember it is God's word which says in *Matthew 3:11; Mark 1:8; Luke 3:16; John 1:32* that Jesus would be the One who would baptise us with the Holy Spirit and with fire. Did God then make a mistake, and did this experience turn out to be a filling only? *Acts 2:4* says: "All of them (the 120) were filled with the Holy Spirit, and began to speak in other tongues as the Holy Spirit enabled them."

Was the baptism then a 'filling' only? Did the total enveloping or immersion of the Holy Spirit turn out to be less than what was promised when it finally came? The meaning of the words as inspired in the original is at stake here. Would we be satisfied with a fish pond if we had bought a farm with a river? Of course not!

As it is "impossible for God to lie" *(Heb 6:18)*, we are assured that we have what He promised. He never makes a mistake. *Acts 2:3* says: "They saw what seemed to be tongues of fire that separated and came to *rest on* each of them." Our Jesus even made the Holy Spirit visible as tongues of fire so that we and they would not doubt this "upon" relationship of the Holy Spirit, even though we cannot see Him. All we need to do is believe God's Word, the same as we did when we heard Jesus knocking at the door of our hearts, pleading to come in.

We read in *Acts 10:44* what happened ten years later: "While Peter was still speaking these words, the Holy Spirit *fell on* all who heard the message." Should we be satisfied with a filling only, when Cornelius and his household had the baptism?

Twenty five years later, in *Acts 19:6*, the twelve men from Ephesus received the same: "When Paul placed his hands on them, the Holy Spirit *came on them*, and they spoke in tongues and prophesied."

All these people had both the filling inside their spirits and a baptism upon them. When we ask for the baptism with the Holy Spirit, this is what we should expect. Picture Him as the Light of God enveloping, filling and remaining upon you, as He did with Jesus.

The following three illustrations show:

1. The sealing with the Holy Spirit when He comes in as God's gift.
2. The infilling with the Holy Spirit when He is given control of your life.
3. The baptism with the Holy Spirit when He comes "upon" one in power for service.

We should obey Jesus' command and receive the baptism without delay.

Sketch no 1 Receiving Christ as Saviour is often pictured as above. People are urged to receive Jesus into their hearts. The man pictured here represents the majority of Christians in the world today. This has led to the mental picture that the Holy Spirit possesses only a small part of our inner beings around our physical hearts.

An unforgiving spirit, some resentment and rebellion, indictated by the black spots, are still clinging to the old nature. In this picture, the Christian possesses the Holy Spirit, but the Holy Spirit is not allowed to possess him.

We are made in the image of God. Let us read *Genesis 1:26–27*: "Then God said, 'Let us make man in our image, in our likeness.' So God created man in His own image, in the image of God He created him."

God repeats this message to us three times. He certainly wants to get it across to us that we are spiritual beings as He is. We are not just body and soul.

We should place the spirit foremost in our thinking. Our spirit is not to be thought of as an impersonal thing in the general area of our hearts. See him as a complete person, as an inner being. Now see what a difference it is going to make if the Holy Spirit fills the whole of our inner being as we see in sketch no 2.

1. We are a spirit
2. We possess a soul i.e. mind, emotion and will
3. We live in a body, which is our earth suit.

Sketch no 2 The Spirit-filled Christian. I trust we are moving away from the mental picture of the spirit of man being confined to an area around the human heart. The spirit is a complete "born again" person inside, reborn by the Holy Spirit, a new creation. The Holy Spirit lives within the reborn human spirit and should be allowed to completely fill and control the spirit, soul and body. The picture is not meant to convey the idea that the spirit has a jagged edge! This is merely a drawing. A better picture is seeing Him as a complete person, say under the first layer of skin, perfect, without blemish or fault. For this to be a reality, the old nature must go. Jesus said the spirit was the "inmost being" *(John 7:38* Living Bible). The Holy Spirit fills us in the "inner being" *(Eph 3:16)* to encompass even the mind, which should also be renewed *(Rom 12:2).*

Without the filling of the Holy Spirit we will not live good lives. This aspect of the Holy Spirit's working within is essential for Christ-like living.

Jesus gave a wonderfully clear picture of what the filling of the Holy Spirit is like *Luke 1:34–36*: "Your eye is the lamp of your body. When your (spiritual) eyes are good, your whole body also is full of light" (What light? Not natural of course – but the Light of God's Spirit.) But when your (spiritual) eyes are bad, your body also is full of darkness. Therefore, if your whole body is full of Light, and no part of it is dark, it will be completely lighted, as when the light of a lamp shines on you."

Sketch no 3 The baptism with the Holy Spirit. The enveloping power of the Holy Spirit is meant, and not the baptism into the body of Christ, whereby all Christians throughout the world become part of Christ's body. We all share in Christ's body, therefore we should not argue this point. The baptism with the Holy Spirit should include the filling with the Holy Spirit as depicted above. It is possible to have the baptism without the filling as with the Corinthian church. They had the gifts associated with the Baptism *(1 Corinthians 1:7)*. But their lives were not becoming as Christians for the most part, were they?

There are eight baptisms in Scripture. We take note of four here.

1. Baptism into Christ's body by the Holy Spirit *(1 Cor 12:13; Rom 6:3; Gal 3:27).*

2. Baptism in water *(Acts 2:38; Rom 6:4)*.

3. Baptism with the Holy Spirit by the Lord Jesus *(Luke 3:16)*.

4. Baptism with suffering *(Luke 12:50; Mark 10:38)*.

Ephesians 4:5 mentions one baptism. This must be the first as it happens to all Christians.

We certainly inherit the Baptism with the Holy Spirit at conversion, so since Jesus commanded it according to *Acts 1:4*, we should claim the inheritance by faith! Do you see the Holy Spirit as being your perfect armour in this picture? It deflects all the fiery darts of the wicked. The Holy Spirit is, in the words of *Ephesians 6:16* "The shield of faith, with which you can extinguish all the flaming arrows of the evil one.

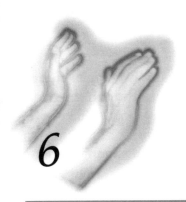

Filled with the Holy Spirit for our interpersonal relationships

6

This important subject is clearly set out in *Ephesians 5:18 to 6:9*. The words there are amplified by God's Word in *Colossians 3:18–4:1*. These scriptures, together with *1 Peter 3:1–9* are the main passages. You will be blessed if you have your own Bible open and mark only the key words that impress you personally.

These scriptures are beautiful for their brief instructions from God on how to relate to one another.

Our relationships with one another (Eph 5:21)

Out of twelve English translations around me, I like the New International Version together with Weymouth's translation of *Ephesians 5:21*. Both are identical. This is what it says: "Submit to one another out of reverence for Christ." Philip's translation says: "Fit in with each other." Moffat says: "Be subject to one another."

All the other versions use the word "submit" or "submitting", so the meaning of these words should leave us in no doubt as to what God wants to say to us. In the Christian life there is to be no lording it over one another. No one orders another as a superior. What is your relationship with others? We are all "brothers" or "sisters" in the Lord, and we are to treat one another with loving respect.

God's instructions to Christians are so short. I marvel at what God has said in one sentence of nine words. "Submit to one another out of reverence for Christ." They deal the death blow to all argument, to the assertion of one's rights. There is no demanding, no shouting, no judging, no condemnation of another. No criticism of a brother or sister. No question of preferring one to another. It is the submission of one to another with mutual respect, and in no way regarding one as inferior to the other. After all, we are all parts of Christ's body. Why are we to behave like this? God gives the reason: out of reverence for our Saviour.

Does the scripture say, "Of course, you all know that wives are excluded from this portion of God's Word?" Many husbands act as though this were the case, as the next verse says, "Wives submit to your husbands." Have we forgotten our marriage vows of: "In honour preferring one another?"

The verse that we are considering is in agreement with this marriage vow, "Submit to one another out of reverence for Christ." There is no room for a woman, under these circumstances, to have a low self-image; no "domineering" wife and no "superior" husband. Man and wife are equals, though each will play a different role, of course.

"Submission" is an attitude of will. It is a decision made by the will. I think we should all pray this prayer:

"Lord, I see what your Word says here. I am going to be submissive in my whole character. I want to be as you say. I am now submitting myself to you, so that through your Holy Spirit living in me, you can work in me a submissive spirit at all times."

I feel that this word on submission must be coupled with *Ephesians 4:32*: "Be kind and compassionate to one another, forgiving each other, just as in Christ God forgave you." Don't these verses dovetail?

In practical Christian living, are these two verses not the key to preventing all divorces? The key to harmonious relations with all Christians? If they are not being put into operation, it is only because we have not sought the filling of the Holy Spirit in this area of our lives. We asked for and have received this in the prayer above.

To complete this picture, let us consider some related scriptures:

- *Galatians 5:13–16:* "You, my brothers, were called to be free. But do not use your freedom to indulge the sinful nature; rather serve one another in love. The entire law is summed up in a single command: Love your neighbour (wife, husband, fellow Christian) as yourself. If you keep on biting and devouring each other, watch out or you will be destroyed by each other. So I say, live by the Spirit (in other words be filled with Him) and you will not gratify the desires of your sinful nature." The brackets are mine.

Doesn't this Word give us the same message?

- *Colossians 3:13* "Bear with each other and forgive whatever grievances (complaints) you may have against another." But how do we do this? How do we rise to this standard? God says, "Not with your love, my child. Throw off your inadequate love and be clothed with Mine." Verse 14 tells us: "And over all these virtues put on (God's) Love which binds us all together in perfect unity."

The Living Bible is worth quoting here, as it strikes a deep chord in our hearts, melting away the hardness which militates against the idea of submission.

- *Colossians 3:13* (LB): "Be gentle and ready to forgive; never hold grudges. Remember the Lord forgave you, so you must forgive others." How do we do it? By loving others. Verse 14: "Let love guide your life, for then the whole church will stay together in perfect harmony."

What church can "split" if God's love is guiding us and putting us into some down-to-earth, practical Christianity? This banishes our pet doctrine for which we would rather die than let God down. After all, we must defend that "doctrine" and mete out some just and ruthless discipline upon the offender!

I know a girl in Christian work who was baptised with the Holy Spirit. Now, she felt, she would be able to work even better for her Lord, because God's Holy Spirit was empowering her. Her experience was no different in kind from that of Jesus in his anointing after He had been baptised in water (*Luke 3:22*). Because of her experience, this girl was dismissed from her work by the Christian director himself. Her friend, the daughter of one of the best known ministers, said, "Then I am resigning too." She did it without hesitation. We dare not mention the name of the Christian organisation as it is well-known world-wide.

At this point I would like to ask whether there isn't a better way? The *phileo* love that we are born with is the kind that acts in the manner we have just seen. There is another love in the Bible called *agape* which we are not born with. It has to be received by faith, as we don't get it automatically. It is actually God's love imparted to us humans, but it only begins to operate when we actively believe in it. This is the kind of love that the Bible describes, in *1 Corinthians 13:4–8*: "Love is patient, love is kind. It does not envy, it does not boast, it is not proud. It is not rude, it is not self seeking, it is not easily angered, it keeps no record of wrongs. Love doesn't delight in evil but rejoices with the truth. It always protects, always trusts, always hopes, always perseveres. Love never fails."

Let us confess this love together: "I am a child of my heavenly Father. I believe I have this love and that this kind God of love will operate in me from now on. It envelopes my whole being through the Holy Spirit and it will never fail!"

There is a call in our day to put away the petty doctrines we hold to so tenaciously. Many of them are based in the tradition of the church and have no foundation in Scripture.

Our attitude should be that found in *1 Peter 4:8*: "Above all, love each other deeply, because love covers a multitude of sins" and in *1 Peter 5:5*: "Young men, in the same way be submissive to those who are older. Clothe yourselves with humility toward one another, because God opposes the proud, but gives grace to the humble." In this regard, see also *1 Peter 3:8*: "Finally all of you live in harmony with one another, be sympathetic, love as brothers, be compassionate and humble."

If the director had had this kind of Christian love in his heart, could he have acted as he did? Before we point a finger at him, we had better be sure that we can point to ourselves as an example of "loving others deeply", of being "clothed with humility toward one another", and of being "compassionate".

Wives and husbands

Ephesians 5:22–24 says: "Wives, submit to your husbands (leadership) as to the Lord. For the husband is the head of the wife as Christ is the Head of the Church, His body, of which He is the Saviour. Now, as the Church submits to Christ, so also wives should submit to their husbands in everything."

There is an order here. First, Jesus is the Head of His body, the Church; second, the husband should be submissive to Jesus as Lord of his life; third, the wife should be submissive both to Jesus as her Lord, and to her husband as her head.

The wife is not to usurp authority over her husband without discussing matters of importance with him first. "Usurp", of course, means to seize a position without a having a right to it.

As I write, my cat is sitting on the table, and I allow her to do this. When she exceeds her privileges and usurps her position by sitting on my open Bible, that is too much! Then she has to be gently reprimanded. One thing is certain. A wife will not achieve any aim by going against what God says here. God will not alter what He has written for our benefit. Usurping authority over the man will achieve nothing for you.

What if your husband is unconverted? *1 Peter 3:1–6* has the answer. The context is that Christ loved us even when we were rebellious against Him, yet his love was so great that He died for us. The Scripture goes on to say, "Wives, in the same way be submissive to your husbands so that, if any of them do not believe the Word, they may be won over without talk (or preaching) by the behaviour of their wives, when they see the purity and reverence of your lives.

"Your beauty should not come from outward adornment, such as braided hair and the wearing of gold jewellery and fine clothes. Instead, it should be that of your inner self, the unfading beauty of a gentle and quiet spirit which is of great worth in God's sight. For this is the way the holy women of the past who put their hope in God used to make themselves beautiful.

"They were submissive to their own husbands, like Sarah, who obeyed Abraham and called him her master. You are her daughters if you do what is right, and do not give way to fear."

Abraham earned the respect of his wife. Men, let us bear this in mind! Wives, be submissive to your unconverted husband. Talk things over as wife to husband if you feel you are being treated unfairly. Men, if we are the men we think we are, we will respect her opinion, won't we? Wives, you won't win your husband to the Lord by preaching, but by your good example.

If you have "fear", that would immediately show up as part of your trouble, as then you do not have much love to submit with, for "Perfect love casts out fear". Men, we should never cause our wives to have fear. We need the filling of the Holy Spirit. *2 Timothy 1:7* says: "I, God, have not given you the Spirit of fear, but of power, and of love, and of a sound mind."

You don't have authority over your husband, but you have power. How? With love, and you don't need to work it up either. Love comes with the filling of the Holy Spirit. How do you remain filled? Use the prayer language often.

How did women in Biblical times make themselves beautiful? By being in the presence of God. This gave them this loving, quiet and gentle spirit. The modern woman of the New Testament can do this more easily than the woman of the Old Testament. Why? Because she has the effortless prayer language. The Holy Spirit knows exactly what to say through you, and Jesus Himself promised you the prayer language in *Mark 16:17*, in these words: "These signs will accompany those who believe: In My name ... They will speak in new tongues."

Make sure you appropriate this priceless gift!

Husbands and wives

The Lord certainly has quite a lot to say to husbands. I don't see anywhere in Scripture that the husband is the law-giver and that he married his wife to have cheap labour. This is often the case, but not according to the Bible. Married life is a loving partnership, not a hell of drudgery for the weaker partner. God has given both husband and wife equality as "Heirs together of the wonderful gift of God's life in you." We are different, but "Vive la difference!"

This is what I read in God's Word, in *1 Peter 3:7*: "Husbands, in the same way (What same way? The way that Jesus loved us so much that He died for us) be considerate as you live with your wife, and treat her with respect as the weaker partner, as heirs together with you of the gracious gift of God's life to you. (Why?) So that God can answer your prayers."

Men, this is a mighty thump from God in one single verse! Who really lays down the line? We, or God? We might have a little authority over our wives, but to what avail if God says, "I won't answer your prayers if you don't love her and show it!" God is saying here: "You are my child. You have been purchased by My Son and you will make it to heaven; but, if you don't treat your wife right, don't expect me to answer your prayers." That hits us where it hurts, doesn't it?

The sooner we begin a deep repentance for the shocking, inconsiderate way we have treated our wives, the sooner we shall become the men of God that He wants us to be.

What does Ephesians say? We have six good verses on the subject there! Let's start with *Ephesians 5:25–33*: "Husbands, love your wives just as Christ loved the church and gave himself up for her, to make her holy, washing her with the cleansing action of the Word of God. This is to present her to Himself as a radiant church, without stain or wrinkle or any other blemish, but holy and blameless. In the same way (that's the standard) husbands ought to love their wives as their own bodies. He who loves his wife loves himself ... Each one of you must love his wife as he loves himself."

Men, to be always belittling ourselves with the notion that we are being modest and humble is not of God. That is the devil's tool to make us useless as servants of the Lord. We should drop that oft-repeated phrase: "I am a sinner saved by grace"; we should rather put our chests out like men, straighten our backs, walk tall, and say to ourselves: "I am a blood-bought child of God, now part of the body of Christ. No longer do I live in sin. I am a son of the King. I have God's Spirit living in me. I do not fear man or the devil. With his Holy Spirit filling me, I have power over sin and authority over the devil. His love flooding over me causes me to love God, my wife, my family, and many others besides. My prayers are answered, because God stops to listen, as I depend on the merits of his dear Son and my Saviour. He respects what I say to Him because I love my wife, and am considerate towards her. I take my turn with things to be done about the house and don't sit around reading the newspaper, expecting to be waited upon hand and foot. Rather, I make time for my children, share their games, joys and sorrows."

A positive confession such as that above, based on the scriptures, will revolutionise our married lives and bring a positive response from our wives and children. It will save one from thoughts or even talk of divorce. Don't get me wrong. I don't say we don't sin. When we do, we should repent quickly and tell God we are sorry. He immediately forgives us if we have forgiven others. God will give us the energy to do all this. With God directing our time, we will be able to help others and pray for them in their need.

"How does God do this for us?" you say. The secret is to use the prayer language all through the day as far as one is able. In this way He keeps one's "battery" charged with his Spirit and builds one up just the way He said He would in 1 *Corinthians 14:4*. The word 'edifies' here is better translated by the modern word 'charges'. He charges us up spiritually and physically, so that we need not feel as tired as we used to do.

Make these strong confessions of the person God wants you to be. You say, "I can't say all that." Well then, you won't have it. God says you have what you say. Do you mean that He says I can? Yes, that is what He says in *Mark 11:23–24* (paraphrased): "I am Jesus, and I tell you the truth. If you look at and brood over your problems, I can't help you. If instead you say boldly to your immediate problem, 'be gone, and be cast into the deep blue sea' and say it with the conviction that you are not going to doubt My Word, with your innermost heart, even though doubts may assail your mind, say it, and that is what you will get. With this conviction in mind, I, Jesus, can say to you, whatever you ask for in prayer, believe that you have already received it and you shall have it."

Give this careful thought. I believe this is what God is actually saying in these verses. If you start confessing negative things, such as "I'm tired", "I don't love my wife as I used to", "I don't have the time to spend with my wife and children", "I must put my business first. After all I am the breadwinner", "I cannot witness, I leave that to the preacher", then all these negative things are exactly what you will get. Can't you make up your mind to confess only positive things? God works only in the positive. It is the devil who works in the negative, and you give ground to him with negative confessions. Negative thoughts and sayings will ruin our lives and marriages. Let us rather confess only positive things, because God says that what we say is what we will have (*Mark 11:23*).

Husbands, this is God's Word to us. If we love our wives as Jesus loves us, our wives will not have difficulty in submitting to us. But there is one warning. We had better never ask our wives to do anything contrary to what God says. Never, for example, forbid her to attend church. Never forbid her to be baptised with God's Holy Spirit. Never forbid her to speak in the prayer language. Never forbid her to love Jesus. All these are the commands of God, so if you ever put yourself above God, you will receive judgement accordingly.

Children

Ephesians 6:1 says: "Children, obey your 'mom' and 'dad' in the Lord, for this is right." *Colossians 3:20* adds: "Obey your parents in everything, for this pleases the Lord." *Ephesians 6:2* continues: "Honour your father and mother, which is the first commandment that carries with it a promise, that it may go well with you, and that you may enjoy a long life on the earth."

Let me ask a question. When do we stop being a child of our parents? Is it when we are thirteen, or when we are twenty-one? My dad died when he was 76. I was at that time a married man with children, but I was still his son. The point I am making is that there is no age when we may start dishonouring our parents, or disobeying them.

If we observe these commands and love our parents, we can live a long, good life. We can claim that promise from the Lord.

Parents

We find directions for parents in *Ephesians 6:4*: "Fathers (and I am sure mothers are included), do not exasperate your children; instead, bring them up in the training and instruction of the Lord." *Colossians 3:21* adds: "Fathers, do not embitter your children, or they will become discouraged."

Is our Christian life one of "don'ts"? God is so positive with us. He encourages us. Even a dog likes encouragement and wags his tail! Let us be determined that, while we will correct our children and never punish them in anger, we will also encourage them and praise them. Our children must grow up with our expression of love.

The car sticker, "Have you hugged your child today?" is an apt one. We must show love and teach him or her to love in return. We must feel their arms in a hug, and they must feel the expression of our love. My father hugged and kissed me until he went home to be with the Lord, and I am glad he did.

Employee/employer relationships

All the translations of *Ephesians 5:5–9* use the words 'slaves' or 'servants'. These two words hardly have an application today. It is the employer/employee relationship that counts.

An employer is entitled to have things his way, providing that this does not cut across what God says. Let us take dishonesty, for instance. If we find ourselves rebelling against legitimate orders or requests from our employer, we should certainly repent, change our attitudes and change our minds. Ask God for both forgiveness and deliverance. There is both cleansing and delivering power in the blood of Jesus, as is clear from *1 John 1:9*: "If we confess our sins, God is faithful and just to forgive us all our sins, and purify us from all unrighteousness."

It is no good leaving a patch of stony ground inside for the devil to work on again. This is like the black spot we referred to before; it remains as a small portion of the devil's property on the perimeter of our spirits. How are we to get rid of it? By repenting, turning away from it with all our hearts and having it removed by the precious blood of Christ. Picture this as having happened by faith, and the Holy Spirit makes it a reality.

We have a reward from God while working for our employers. How can this be? Well, it is all here in this passage of scripture. "Serve wholeheartedly, as if you were serving the Lord, not men, and because you know that the Lord will reward everyone for whatever good he does, whether he is a slave or free" (*Eph 6:7*).

Working this way brings tremendous joy. You not only get a monthly cheque from your firm but, even more important, an eternal reward! All we have to do is to work as if we were working for Jesus. *Colossians 3:17, 23–24* confirms this: "And whatever you do, whether it is what you say or do (on holiday, at work or at home) do it all in the name of the Lord Jesus, giving praise and thanks to the Father through Him. Whatever you do, work at it with all your heart, as working for the Lord, not for man, since you know that you will receive an inheritance from the Lord as a reward. It is the Lord, (the Messiah) you are serving."

This gives us tremendous incentive in our ordinary work. One's work is never a burden, and great joy floods one's soul as one realises again and again that one is doing something for one's Saviour.

Employers

Ephesians 6:9 (LB) says: "And you slave-owners (employers) must treat your slaves (employees) correctly, just as I have told them to treat you. Don't keep threatening them. Remember, you yourselves are slaves to Christ. You have the same Master as they have, and He has no favourites."

This Scripture is so plain it needs no comments. I have been asking the Lord what to say, and He has said to me that I must testify to what He did for me when I was furniture manager in a large departmental store in the centre of town. There was constant disagreement and ill-feeling amongst the sales staff. I had pressure put on me from all sides – delivery and other sources of problems, the phone constantly ringing, harassment all round. I asked the Lord what I should do. He said, "Start a prayer meeting with the staff before you start work." This was a hard thing to do, but it was made a little easier when Kevin, another Christian who was a manager in another department, agreed to join us.

The sales staff suddenly realised what Christianity was all about. Some were encouraged to make an open stand for Christ. The atmosphere became sweet and pleasant. We began taking authority against all action of the enemy, such as through the phone, inexplicable damage to furniture, harassment and pressure. What a change! Instead of pressure enough to split the head, there was joy welling up in my heart, bringing a deep inward peace.

Anyone in charge can do this, and his authority can count for God. God knows this, and prospers the business, too. All Christians have authority. We inherited it from Jesus. In *Luke 10:19* Jesus said: "I have given you authority ... to overcome all the power of the enemy. Nothing will harm you."

Again *Matthew 28:18–19* says "All authority in heaven and on earth has been given to Me. Therefore go making disciples of all nations." This delegated authority from Jesus Himself is useless unless we take courage and use it.

In the next chapter, God speaks again from the pages of Ephesians to show us how authority over the enemy will become a reality.

P.S. How to save your marriage in 30 days!

1. Renounce your love as inadequate for this task.
2. Take God's agape love by faith, true love is not a feeling, it is a decision.
3. Command all spirits of lack of love, hate, unforgiveness, adultery, rebellion and criticism to go in Jesus' name.
4. Ask God to restore your marriage, to bring you and your wife to unity and completeness again.
5. Affirm that your body is reserved only for the Holy Spirit, and not for the devil's rubbish.
6. Every morning take your partner a cup of tea in bed, give her a hug and say "I love you darling". Do this even if you don't get a response for 30 days. If you do it with God's imparted love you will not fail!

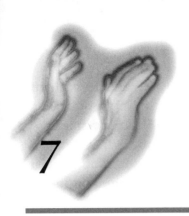

Putting on the armour of God

7

We as Christians can be fully clothed with the armour of God. The question is: Are we automatically clothed with God's armour? Because we are saved, do we automatically have a helmet of salvation? Apparently not. The Word states that we are to *put on the full armour of God.*

Let us read the whole passage as we find it in *Ephesians 6:10–18*. "Finally, be strong in the Lord and in His mighty power. Put on the whole armour of God so that you can take your stand against the devil's schemes, for our struggle is not against flesh and blood (people), but against the rulers, against the authorities, against the powers of this dark world, and against the spiritual forces of evil in the heavenly realms." (Living Bible: "Huge numbers of wicked spirits in the spirit world.")

Because we do not see these spirits, it does not mean that they are not there. God is affirming in this scripture that they are there: "Therefore, put on the whole armour of God, so that when the day of evil comes, you may be able to stand your ground and, after you have done everything, to stand.

Stand firm then, with the belt of truth buckled round your waist, with the breastplate of righteousness in place, and with your feet fitted with readiness that comes from the gospel of peace. In addition to all this, take up the shield of faith, with which you can extinguish all the flaming arrows of the evil one. Take the helmet of salvation and the sword of the Holy Spirit, which is the Word of God. And pray in the Spirit on all occasions with all kinds of prayers and requests. With this in mind, be alert and always keep on praying for all saints."

Karl Barth said something like this: "Jesus has overcome the devil, therefore we should ignore him as if he doesn't exist." Well, the Church of Jesus Christ has done this for too long. We cannot ignore our enemy. We have to defeat him! The passage we have read tells us that Christians find themselves in a spiritual war against the powers of darkness. One never gets a balanced view by taking only a part of scripture. Doctrine comes from studying scripture as a whole.

1 Peter 5:8 tells us: "Your enemy, the devil, prowls around like a roaring lion, looking for someone to devour. Resist him." *James 4:7* says: "Submit yourselves to God. Resist the devil and he will flee from you." These words were written many years after Jesus died on the cross, where He defeated the devil for us. *Colossians 2:15* emphasise this "And having disarmed the powers and authorities, He made a public spectacle of them, triumphing over them by the Cross."

This is Good News. We have a disarmed enemy. If we don't win against the enemy, it must be because we don't have our armour on. In *John 10:10*, Jesus said of the devil, "He has come to steal, to kill and to destroy." To achieve this, he will use all unfair means, and we can't stand without armour. We should be binding him, and keeping him bound. If we allow the devil to bind us in our witness for Christ and keep us fearful, we cannot release ourselves, let alone launch out to help and release.

In *Luke 13:16* Jesus refers again to the devil: "Then should this woman, a daughter of Abraham, whom Satan has kept bound for eighteen long years, be set free on the Sabbath day from what bound her?" Jesus wants to set us free, so that we in turn can become a blessing to others, and do what Jesus did. *Acts 10:38* indicates that Jesus made constant war against the devil during those three years after He was baptised with the Holy Spirit: "How God anointed Jesus of Nazareth with the Holy Spirit and power, and how He went around doing good and healing all who were oppressed under the power of the devil, because God was with Him." Our instruction is found in *John 14:12*: "I tell you the truth; anyone who has faith in Me will do what I am doing."

Our victory is not achieved by ignoring the devil. This way he will oppress, steal from, kill and destroy us. Our victory is to have the same baptism and anointing that Jesus had, to triumph over the devil in every attack he makes upon us, to go about doing good and helping others to get free from the severe pressure they are under from the devil.

Study *Luke 11:22*: "When someone stronger attacks and overpowers a strong man, he takes away the armour in which the man trusted and divides up the spoils."

Brothers and sisters, we now realise with great joy that Jesus has disarmed our enemy. The devil has no armour! It is we who have the armour on by faith, and we are the winners in every confrontation!

We are now going to consider what each item of our armour is and how to ensure that we have it on. For easy memorisation, we shall start at the head and move to the toes. Then we shall consider the weapons as well.

The helmet of salvation

Does this mean that when we have the assurance of salvation we automatically have the helmet on? To answer this question we must turn to another Scripture which tells us more about this part of the armour.

1 Thessalonians 5:8–11 says: "But since we belong to the day, let us be self-controlled, putting on faith and love as a breastplate, and the hope of salvation as a helmet. For God did not appoint us to suffer wrath (violence, fury, from another being) but to receive salvation through our Lord Jesus Christ. He died for us so that, whether we are awake or asleep (the helmet will be there) we may live together with Him. Therefore encourage one another, and build each other up."

This hope of salvation worn as a helmet referred to in the last verse is so sure because it is linked with faith. This is the kind of hope that never condemns others, but rather encourages others. This hope "charges" others up so that they start enjoying life in the power of the Holy Spirit. Being linked with faith, this hope is so sure that it knows that the helmet will not vanish while one is asleep!

The other kind of hope does not lead to faith. It says, "I will live as best I can. When I die, I shall be thrown on the mercy of God. I hope He will receive me." This hope ignores Jesus, for verse 9 says, "to receive salvation through our Lord Jesus Christ." There is no hope if we reject God's way of salvation, that is, through his Son. The Helmet of Hope is put on by faith in our Lord Jesus. We can't physically put it on, of course. What we picture is what we believe! We picture it on us day and night, made a reality through the Holy Spirit upon us. It protects the head, neck and face, because it has its visor down!

If you feel miserable and are usually more down than up, start thanking God for your salvation in Jesus. Your spirit will rise up with joy, and you will be buoyant with *hope*. Here is the crowning verse for you: "May the God of hope fill you with all joy and peace as you trust in Jesus, so that you may overflow with *hope* by the power of the Holy Spirit" (Rom 15:13).

What about *1 Thessalonians 5:9*? This verse is in the context of the helmet of hope through salvation: "For God did not appoint us to suffer wrath, but to receive salvation through our Lord Jesus Christ." A few of the translations in front of me imply that this "wrath" would come from God. But we are now in the era of the New Testament, which means, of course, that we are under God's grace and love. The only wrath we could expect would come from the devil. Every Christian should take authority over this kind of wrath – violence, fury – from another, the devil, in the name of Jesus.

In this time of increasing persecution, Christians should not accept violence and fury against themselves without binding the unseen spirit forces in the power of Jesus' name. This is our hope, and this is our right as we are told in *Hebrews 6:19* "We have this hope as an anchor for the soul, firm and secure."

What is this hope which we have upon us as a helmet? *Colossians 1:27* talks of "this mystery, which is Christ in you the *hope* of glory." This leads us on to the next part of our armour.

The breastplate of righteousness

The breastplate of righteousness covers both the front and back. We certainly do not wear it by self-effort, but by Christ who is our righteousness. If we have longed and prayed for a holy life, doing all in our own power to achieve it, we may as well stop now!

Martin Luther tried this before us, harder perhaps than anyone I have read of. Every new effort of his ended in failure. Surely he would receive it in the holy city of Rome, he thought. While he was climbing the seven holy steps on his knees, imploring God to impart righteousness to him, the voice of God came as clearly as if it were audible: "The righteousness of God is by faith of Jesus Christ unto all, and upon all them that believe." Martin Luther turned to see who was behind him, but to his surprise there was no one. The voice of God had spoken to him. He never got to the top step. He rose up and walked down, a believer in the righteousness of Christ imparted to him by faith. The Reformation had begun! Let us consider a number of verses in this regard:

1 Thessalonians 5:8: "Putting on the breastplate of faith and love." Righteousness is not a rigid set of rules that have to be obeyed. It is our Saviour living within us. We listen to his voice and obey Him with faith and love. The issue of faith is love. This is where I prefer the Living Bible. Look at the following references emphasising love, obedience and faith as part of this breastplate:

John 14:15, 21: "If you love me, obey me. The one who obeys Me is the one who loves Me ... and I will reveal Myself to him."

Isn't this what the Christian desires above all? To be in the inner circle of

Jesus' friends and witness his revelation. Now you know the secret, love and obedience.

John 14:22–23: "Judas (not Iscariot) said: 'Sir, are you going to reveal yourself only to us disciples and not to the world at large? Jesus replied: 'I will only reveal Myself to those who love and obey Me. Anyone who does not obey Me doesn't love Me.'"

This is true righteousness: just loving and obeying Jesus. It is not hard to hear his voice, and as you obey it you hear it louder each day. The same message is found in *John 10:27*: "My sheep listen to my voice. I know them and they follow Me." Finally *Romans 3:22* tells us that, "This righteousness from God comes through faith in Jesus Christ to all who believe."

Let me tell a story of how the breastplate works, of how the enemy tries to find a gap in our armour and manoeuvres to make us drop our breastplates of faith and love.

A dear saint of God, a lady greatly used by God in personal work, one day suddenly had a pain which stretched from her back to the front of her chest. At night, the pain was so bad that she could not lie down in her bed, but had to sleep in a reclining chair. Christian friends prayed the prayer of faith for her, but nothing happened. Her husband took her to specialist after specialist, to no avail.

My great friend in the Lord, Kobus Geldenhuys, who was greatly used in the healing ministry, prayed for her. Still nothing happened. More than six months later, in January, Kobus was praying for some other people in her home, when suddenly he saw in a vision what the trouble was. Three arrows had been fired into her from the back. Two protruded slightly from the front and one of these was touching the base of her heart. Preposterous, you say! Just because we cannot see something with the natural eye, must we regard it as unreal? If we open ourselves to the gifts of the Spirit, God can speak to all of us in these ways.

In this case God had spoken more effectively in a vision than in words. Kobus felt that they should demonstrate the action of pulling out the arrows by faith. This they did, one, two, three ... and the pain of seven months was gone. Do you see how the vision above became a "Word of knowledge" when Kobus told what he saw? This small portion of God's knowledge brought the "gift of faith" into operation, which is so essential before a healing or miracle. The gifts of the Holy Spirit are incredibly precious!

This lady recollected how her breastplate had been let down. She was ministering to some women, praying for their needs after a home meeting.

Then she overheard some of them whispering, "There she goes again. She always thinks she is so holy that she must always be praying for everyone else." She went on as if she had not heard, but the unkind words drove home like a dagger. She felt resentful toward these women. Shortly afterwards, she completely forgot about the incident, but on reflection she knew that this was the time when the pain started. She now confessed her resentment to the Lord and extended forgiveness to the women whom she did not know. Thus another part of the old nature was removed, where a foothold was given to the devil. She is being used by the Lord more than ever. Praise God!

A thing like this can happen so easily to any one of us. A certain person in our church suffered daily from headaches. Prayer brought about a slight relief, but a few of us decided that we must hear from God if we were to help this dear child of God. Using the prayer language, we expressly asked the Lord for help, and immediately I could see a black tapered shaft protruding into the head. As I touched the spot, I heard the reply, "That's it." When I explained what I saw to the others, this became "a word of knowledge" to us all. The next gift, "the gift of faith" rose up in our hearts, and we simply made the actions of pulling out the shaft by faith. As we did so, the pain left. What a relief this was from that oppressive headache!

I asked the Lord what this shaft was, and what those three arrows of the previous case were? He said, "Such are the fiery darts of the Wicked One." So we constantly need God's armour, and we need the shield of faith to stop all the darts of the Wicked One.

Since the shield is held in place by an arm, we should consider the shield as the next part of the armour of God.

The shield of faith

What part of the body does the shield protect? The answer is the whole of the body. Who operates this spiritual shield? Only the Holy Spirit can. Faith is the link which sets the shield in operation. We cannot even see the darts of the Wicked One being fired! The Holy Spirit sees the darts. He is also the One who holds the shield for us. But the Holy Spirit can only manipulate the shield in response to our faith. *Hebrews 11:6* says: "Without faith it is impossible to please God." God said to Abraham in *Genesis 15:1*: "I am thy shield and thy exceeding great reward." The knowledge that we are of Abraham's seed should be reason for contentment, not so? We read in *Galatians 4:28*: "We brothers, like Isaac, are children of the promise." David said in *2 Samuel 22:3, 36*: "God is my shield and the horn of my salvation ... You give me your shield of victory." *Psalm 3:3* tells us that "You are a shield around me, O Lord." I like that, don't you?

As a result of the baptism of the Holy Spirit, we have Him all around us. You can choose to have Him all around you, or not, as you will. It is a matter of faith. All I can say is that I have never known such victory over the devil as when I am conscious of the shield around me, nor such a joy in my Christian life. Nor have I felt such a spirit of worship toward my God as I have since I was baptised, or immersed, with the Holy Spirit. I would not give up my shield for anything!

The Spirit is holding it all the time, and I do not need to hold on to it.

The skirt of truth

Some of the translations use the word "belt" of truth. But it is not such a narrow piece of armour as a belt. It covers the body from the breastplate down to the knees, just as the Roman soldier wore it. The greater the protection the better, and that should be our picture of the skirt.

The picture I see is that the Holy Spirit is my girdle of truth. *John 16:13* says: "The Spirit of *truth* ... He will guide you into all truth" and *Ephesians 5:9* (KJ) tells us that "The fruit of the Spirit is in all goodness and righteousness and truth."

If we fall into error, we lose the skirt of truth and we are immediately vulnerable. We lay ourselves open to believing a lie from the devil. The thoughts I am putting on paper have been constantly confirmed by other believers, for the Truth belongs to the full body of believers and not only to a section. Any new thought will have the witness of other believers, to confirm its truth.

My prayer is, "Lord, guard these pages from error, and let them be filled with Your truth." Many of the thoughts which you will find in these pages may be a little different from what you have been used to, so constantly ask the Lord, "Is this truly what the Bible teaches?" Do not reject truth out of hand because it is not what you have heard before, or because your church does not teach it.

Do you have problems with sex? This will most certainly be because you have not donned the skirt of truth. Instead, you tend to dwell on untruthful images of sex which the devil brings. God's Word commands us in *2 Corinthians 10:5* to make every thought captive to the obedience of Christ. Repent of succumbing to this temptation of the devil and get it out of your system. Victory in all personal and private areas of your life is essential. Fail here and you will not be able to launch out in your "Gospel shoes".

The gospel shoes

These shoes cover the feet and legs to the knees, but are made light, like those of the Roman soldier, so as not to impede the spreading of the Gospel of Salvation and Peace. I rather like the King James version here. This is what it says in *Ephesians 6:15*: "And your feet shod with the preparation of the Gospel of Peace." I have often asked myself the question: Why are people not very confident about taking the Gospel to others, even if they are Spirit-filled? I do believe the Lord has provided the Hatfield Community in Pretoria with a significant answer. One of our pastors, Reverend Keith Lee, now gone to be with the Lord, wrote two books on the subject for use as training manuals. His whole aim was to train Christians in what to say to others. This 17-week course includes training on how to lead a soul to the Lord, and to lead him on further to become a disciple of Jesus.

Students of this course, after studying two-thirds of it, often go to a shopping centre in the evening. Being led by the Holy Spirit, they may go up to a total stranger, knowing exactly what to say, and end up leading the person to Christ within an hour.

What has happened? These people have put on their gospel shoes! When they start speaking, they know where they are going. They have the whole plan of salvation in their minds, complete with at least 40 verses which the Holy Spirit can call to their mind to suit each individual case.

Taking the course made a profound difference to my own life. I am filled with a zeal for making disciples for Jesus. Why? Because I have no fear about what I am going to say, and other students will say the same. More than 3000 members have been trained in this way so far. The method is that a person who has been through the course trains two more. The ultimate aim is to train the whole church. Other churches are trained upon invitation. Pastors are trained in a concentrated six-day course.

This is the day of great spiritual harvest. We should see to it that we are trained to put on this part of the armour. The Scripture says, "Your feet shod with the preparation of the gospel of peace." Preparation is called for. Can you rightly claim to have on this part of the armour when you have not trained yourself to lead others to his Saviour? Challenging, isn't it?

More will be said about training yourself in "the preparation of the gospel of peace", in learning to use the Sword of the Spirit.

The sword of the Spirit

There are two weapons of attack in the armour. The sword is one of these. The other can be found in *Ephesians 6:18*: "Praying in the Spirit." As I am saying this, I am wondering if there are not three weapons of attack. Are not the Gospel Shoes for the proclamation of the Good News also an attacking weapon? These are for going right into the enemy's territory to pull out converts to Jesus Christ. I am not saying that "the Sword of the Spirit – the Word of God" cannot be used in defence. Jesus Himself used it in his temptation. Primarily, we need to use the sword in attack.

"The sword of the Spirit which is the Word of God" is constantly used in leading others to Christ. How can a young Christian, who has not had the opportunity of getting to know the Bible, use the "Sword of the Spirit"? This is what I suggest. Your testimony counts for a great deal. In your witness to others, start with your testimony. You do not relate how bad you have been, but your testimony must be of Jesus. Jesus could put things into few words and we will not improve on what He said in *Acts 1:8:* "But ye shall receive power after that the Holy Spirit has come upon you, and ye shall be witnesses unto Me." You won't get off the ground without the baptism of the Holy Spirit. Jesus Himself was baptised with the Holy Spirit before His public ministry. The next step is to witness what Jesus has done for you. Write out your testimony, and make sure that it glorifies Jesus. Make it short, no longer than 5 minutes, and see that it contains three steps: Before, Then, Now.

Jesus believed in a testimony. The testimony of one man opened up a whole country to receive Jesus' subsequent ministry as we read in *Mark 5:18–20:* "As Jesus was getting into the boat, the man who had been demon possessed begged to go with him. Jesus did not let him, but said, 'Go home to your family, and tell them how much the Lord has done for you, and how He has had mercy on you.' So the man went away and began to tell in the ten cities of his country how much Jesus had done for him. And all the people were amazed."

If he had preached at them, all the people would have been antagonised. *Do not preach!*

What was the result of this man's testimony? The answer lies in *Mark 6:54–55.* Remember these people had chased Jesus away. Now this is what happened on his second visit: "As soon as they got out of the boat, people recognised Jesus. They ran throughout that whole region and carried the sick on mats to wherever they heard He was."

Your testimony

What was your worst problem before you came to know Jesus? Start with that, and do not relate a history of your past.

Make it something like this: "Before I met Jesus, my best friend was killed in a motor accident and this made me think about God and the hereafter. Before I met Jesus, I had a terrible temper. Then I heard that Jesus could change my life. I decided to give Him a chance to do this for me. Now He has proved He can do this in my life. (A testimony in twenty seconds!)

Here is an example of my own testimony and how I could use it to bring someone to Christ. You can use this as a basis for training yourself to lead a person to Christ. The key question we were taught on the course opens up the conversation, giving you the opportunity to lead the person to Christ. I am simplifying the approach to make it easy for you to put on your sword and gospel shoes.

"Before I met Jesus, I noticed a wonderful change had come over my sister. She said it was Jesus who had made the change. I thought I would like a similar change in my own life, so I determined to find out how Jesus could change me. Then I met Him. (Don't tell how you met Him at this stage.) Now He is busy changing my life, and I am amazed at how my life is not full of emptiness anymore. Now I know that I'll go to be with Him in heaven when I die.

"May I ask you a question?"

"Yes."

"Do you think you will go to heaven when you die?" (Ask this pleasantly and with a smile.) "Well, I hope so." This leaves the person open for the next step. "May I share with you how I came to know Jesus, and how you can know Him, too?"

"Yes. You seem so sure, it would be interesting to find out."

"Well, it happened this way. I was reading in the last book of the Bible. (Take out your New Testament and open it at *Revelation 3:15*: 'I know your deeds, that you are neither cold nor hot. I wish you were one or the other. So, because you are lukewarm, I will spue you out of my mouth.'

"That gave me quite a shock. It was like God speaking directly to me. Do you also feel that you would not like God to spue you out of his mouth?"

"Yes."

"Then I found that God wanted me to turn from the way I was living, as He says in v. 19: 'Be in earnest then, and turn from your sins.' I then realised that Jesus was knocking at the door of my heart, as He says in the next verse: 'Listen! I stand at the door and knock. If anyone hears my voice, I will come into him.' I realised that Jesus wanted to come into my heart and life, and that I should open up to Him." (Now in your Bible next to *Revelation 3:20* put this reference: *1 John 1:9* – then you will always know where to turn to next.) 'If we confess our sins God is faithful and just to forgive us our sins and to purify us from all unrighteousness.' Next to this verse put *Romans 10:9* (1) 'If you confess with your mouth that Jesus is Lord (of your life) (2) and believe in your heart that God raised Him from the dead, (3) you will be saved.' "Well, I did not find it hard to believe that God raised Jesus from the dead. It would be no good believing a dead Jesus, would it?"

"No."

"So you also believe that God raised Jesus from the dead?"

"Yes, because I see it here."

"It remains then for you to confess Jesus with your mouth, to confess that He is Lord, and that you will put Him first in your life. I guess that in your heart of hearts you would like to do that, wouldn't you?"

"Yes, I would."

"Would you like to pray yourself, or would you like to pray after me and so open your heart and life to Jesus?"

"I would prefer to pray after you."

"Pray this prayer after me then: My Father in heaven, I don't want you to spue me out of your mouth. I do want to repent and turn from the way I am living right now. I have heard that Jesus is knocking at the door of my heart, and I open myself to Him. I confess all my sins to you, and ask you to forgive me. I ask you to purify me from all unrighteous acts, and to fill the emptiness of my life with your Spirit. No longer do I want to control my own life. I ask the Lord Jesus to be Lord and King in my life. Thank you, Lord Jesus, that according to your promise you have come in to live within me by your Spirit. Amen."

"How do you know that Jesus has come to live in you?"

"Because I read it in the Bible."

"Well answered. We know because God promised this in his Word, not because we feel so. If the devil were to come to us and say, 'Well, you don't feel as if Jesus is in you, do you'? What would you answer him? The Bible says He is in me in *Revelation 3:20*. You are then using an attacking weapon which the devil cannot withstand.

Here we have seen only the basics in leading someone to Jesus. As few verses as possible have been used. If you use this guide and start practising it, you will be able to expand on it. Under the Holy Spirit's guidance, you will become a very proficient wielder of the Sword of the Spirit.

Praying in the Spirit

Ephesians 6:18 says: "And pray in the Spirit on all occasions, with all kinds of prayers and requests. With this in mind, be alert and always keep on praying for all the saints."

What does praying in the Spirit mean? For some of us will be shocked to find out that it is praying in "tongues". I prefer to call it "prayer language". *1 Corinthians 14:2* says, "For anyone who speaks in a tongue does not speak to men but to God." Of course, when we are speaking to God, we usually call it prayer, don't we? Hence the "prayer language".

I had a bias against "tongues" and I guess many of us have. Lay aside any bias you may feel for the moment. Come to God with an open mind. Accept that if God says it, you will receive what He says in the matter. Do you agree?

Jesus was the first to give us a clue as to what God was going to introduce in this day of grace of the New Testament. Let us read what He said to the woman of Samaria in *John 4:23–24*: "Yet a time is coming and now is when the true worshippers will worship the Father (firstly) in spirit, and (secondly) in truth. For they are the kind of worshippers the Father seeks. God is Spirit, and His worshippers must worship Him in spirit and in truth." In two ways, do you see? In the spirit and in truth.

1 Corinthians 14:14–15 tells us: "For if I pray in a tongue, my spirit prays, but my mind is unfruitful. So what shall I do? I will pray with my spirit, but I will also pray with my mind. I will sing with my spirit, but I will also sing with my mind." The Amplified Bible is even clearer. It emphasises that my spirit through the Holy Spirit living inside will be doing the praying.

This statement is so different from what we are used to that at first it is hard to grasp. The most common response is: "My church has never said this! They say 'tongues' was only for the primitive church. Its practice ceased long ago!" All this is, of course, the devil's lie. God's Word says nothing of the kind. It says in *1 Corinthians 13:8* (KJ): "tongues shall cease, whether there be knowledge, it shall vanish away." Has knowledge vanished? Neither has tongues. I stand as a testimony to that, together with millions of other Christians.

We do well to remember that Paul is not really speaking from these pages. This is God's Word to us. *1 Corinthians 14:5* informs us: "I would like everyone of you to speak in tongues." In *1 Corinthians 14:18* Paul says of himself, "I thank God I speak in tongues more than all of you." That is privately, of course. It is the prayer weapon for the individual to use in private. God knows what He is about. He knows we cannot see into the spiritual world. We can't see when Satan is about to attack. The Holy Spirit can see this and if we pray in the "prayer language", He directs the prayer to defeat Satan's attack.

He is not limited like our poor finite minds. He knows everything that is happening in advance. He can prevent many bad things happening to us if we admit that He knows more than we do. Let Him give you the strange words to pray which you don't understand with your mind. The prayer language is the attacking weapon in your armour that God wants you to use. Don't lay your best weapon aside. There is no truth in the rumour that you can't have "the prayer language". Jesus Himself said that you can have it in *Mark 16:17*: "And these signs will accompany (whom?) those who believe. In My Name they ... will speak in new tongues." Yes, it is amazing what you can do in the authority of Jesus' name! You too, in his name, can start using the "prayer language".

I heard someone say, "But I thought Paul said 'I would rather speak five intelligible words to instruct others than ten thousand words in a tongue'." The Word of God says in *1 Corinthians 14:19*, "But in the church I would rather speak five intelligible words to instruct others, than ten thousand words in a tongue." The prayer language is limited in church by strict instruction. *1 Corinthians 14:27–28* says: "If anyone speaks in a tongue, two, or at the most three, should speak, one at a time, and someone must interpret. If there is no interpreter, the speaker should keep quiet in the church, and speak to himself and God." In other words, pray silently as much as you like, for then you will be speaking to God. You are in a church full of people, most of whom are unknown to you. You may feel an urge to pray for others present.

In your own language it is impossible to pray with any accuracy for individuals, but in the prayer language you can. You can sit there praying silently in the Spirit. This prayer has tremendous value. Why? Because the Holy Spirit knows each one individually and in intimate detail. His prayer prayed through our lips has far greater value than any general prayer we could offer.

This is the marvellous inherent power of the Holy Spirit's gift, called "praying in the Spirit". It is the secret weapon every Christian should use privately all through the day. Picture Paul using this gift while making tents, while walking along dusty roads. Picture yourself using this prayer language while driving your car, mowing the lawn, and even while you are doing general work for your firm. Once you get into it, this language flows, even when you are writing. How can this be? It does not originate in the mind. You don't need to think or concentrate on what you are saying. Only our Heavenly Father could have thought of an attacking weapon like this, and of giving it to us as a gift!

What if friends phone because of some upheaval at work or in a fit of depression and ask for help? In circumstances like these you should pray together and take authority over the enemy in the name of Jesus, for the enemy is at the root of the trouble. This you have to do in your own language.

Then I would like to stress that we pray in the prayer language to cover everything that we cannot know or understand in the situation. Impossible situations are dealt with in the Lord's wisdom, for He knows what is best in every situation.

Since using the "prayer language" in my ordinary work situation, I can honestly say I have never had a bad day. We will not be immune from trouble. Neither was Paul. He was stoned and left for dead, yet he was able to get up and go back to his friends. In terrible storms at sea, even when shipwrecked, there was no loss of life. Paul and Silas, when thrown into prison and scourged, were delivered from an impossible position. Good was brought out of it, because the jailer and his family were brought to the Lord. Never blame God for any evil that may befall you, for God cannot do evil. The devil is behind every evil circumstance in your life, yet God can bring good out of evil, as we see in *Romans 8:28* (Living Bible): "And we know that all that is happening to us is working for our good, if we love God, and are fitting into His plans."

In these days of great pressure and little rest, we must get away from the idea that the only place to pray is at our bedside and on our knees. God is far more practical than that. Suppose you get thrown out of your routine and miss your quiet time with the Lord. Are you going to stand accused before Satan who will tell you that everything is now going to go wrong for you? Your secret weapon is the answer! You will carry on praying all day, your tongue moving silently and your inner ear hearing the flow of the prayer language.

I had a strong bias against the prayer language. I had to repent for despising God's gift. You, who have had a bias against "tongues" and who may even have that bias now, don't presume to be wiser than the Holy Spirit, as He is the one who gives the utterance. Remember that all gifts from the Holy Spirit are wonderful. All his gifts, and not only some, are at our disposal when we reach out to Him, and He decides which one we need at the moment of need.

Ephesians 6:18 says: "And pray in the Spirit on all occasions." Do you see

66

any option in this? I don't hear God saying, "If you have not yet launched out into the prayer language which I have given you, then I absolve you from this instruction." What God says, stands. He is not going to alter anything for our benefit.

His instructions to all his children are to "Take the full armour of God" and "Pray in the Spirit on all occasions with all kinds of prayers and requests." When you sense an authoritative prayer is needed, pray in Jesus' name. When you feel that the enemy must be bound, use that prayer. When you feel in your spirit that a request to your Heavenly Father is required, frame that request in the spirit, through the wisdom of the indwelling Holy Spirit.

There is one very beneficial side-effect to the prayer language and that is what *Ephesians 6:18* says about keeping alert and fresh: "Be alert, and always keep on praying – in the Spirit – for all the saints."

Your prayer has to be "in the Spirit", because we know so few of the saints! The side-effect is that, while one uses the prayer language, one is physically energised.

The whole armour of God is actually the Holy Spirit upon us, clothing us with Himself. Picture Him upon you, enveloping you with his armour of light. What you picture is what you believe; what you believe becomes reality. He is upon you night and day, and He does not leave you when you are asleep.

Life in the Spirit is a wonderful life, and Jesus lived it before us. The next chapter goes on to show how the Holy Spirit was operative in the life of Jesus, so don't diminish the work of the Holy Spirit in your life.

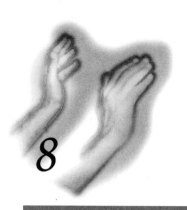

The Holy Spirit in the life of Jesus

8

When was Jesus filled with the Holy Spirit? Was it after his baptism with water? A number of biblical references provide clues to these questions:

Luke 4:1 says: "Jesus full of the Holy Spirit returned from the Jordan and was led by the Spirit in the desert." Was this the first time that Jesus was filled with the Holy Spirit? Had He lived for 30 years without sin, unaided, and in his own strength? Had he lived his life up to this point without the aid of the Holy Spirit? These are all valid questions, and they require an answer.

Luke 1:15 refers to John the Baptist: "For he will be great in the sight of the Lord, and he will drink no wine or liquor, and he will be filled with the Holy Spirit while yet in his mother's womb."

Would God have given his Son an inferior experience to John the Baptist? Surely this is unthinkable. In *Luke 1:35* the angel Gabriel while speaking to Mary says of the infant Jesus: "The Holy Spirit will come upon you, and the power of the Most High will overshadow you; and for that reason the holy offspring shall be called the Son of God." The Living Bible puts it more strongly: "so the baby born to you will be utterly holy – the Son of God." Was the baby then utterly holy in his own strength?

Did the Holy Spirit have a part to play in such a holy life? Can you imagine the Holy Spirit, when He had planted the seed in Mary's womb, saying: "Now, sorry little Life, when you are born, and over the years as you grow into manhood, you are on your own. You are to be left to your own devices, but you are never to sin. According to the Father's instructions I can only come back to assist you when you are 30 years old. When you are weakest and during your formative years I shall unfortunately not be here to help you." Such an idea seems ludicrous, doesn't it?

It is also unscriptural. The Father, Jesus and the Holy Spirit can never be separated since They are one. The only time this did actually happen was the brief moment on the Cross when the Father had to withdraw Himself from his Son as the filth of the world's sin was deliberately carried by Jesus. It was our sin that forced Him to withdraw from his Son. *Hebrews 9:14* says: "Christ, who through the eternal Spirit offered Himself unblemished to God."

In the meantime Elizabeth's son John was born, and the people of these Judean hills said of him, "What then is this child going to be? For the Lord's hand was with him" (*Luke 1:66*). Do we see that John did not become the great man he was without the Holy Spirit? Of course, we know that, despite being a great man, he was still a sinner.

What about Jesus? Was Jesus able to live his perfect life without the assistance of the Holy Spirit during his early years, even though He was the perfect man and God, 100 % man and 100 % God? Of course not. It is unthinkable that Jesus should be separated from the Father and the Holy Spirit, except as mentioned above. We might ask whether He was not inherently good, being God? He denied this in *Luke 18:18*: "'Why do you call Me good?' Jesus answered 'No one is good – except God alone.'"

Jesus further said in *John 4:10*: "The words I say to you are not just my own. Rather it is the Father living in Me, who is doing His work." The Father lived in Him through the Holy Spirit, as Jesus lives in us through the Holy Spirit.

Now a key word, hitherto unnoticed, is used in *Luke 4:1* for the filling of the Holy Spirit: "Jesus, full of the Holy Spirit." There is a less common word for "full" in the New Testament: *pleres*. This Greek word means that his filling was perfect, that He was permeated with the Holy Spirit, an experience that was never to be repeated. His filling did not have its commencement at the river Jordan. Jesus, like John the Baptist, was filled with the Holy Spirit even before his birth. Now He had a new experience of the Holy Spirit when, as it says in *Luke 3:21–22*: "Jesus was baptised too, and as He was praying, heaven opened and the Holy Spirit descended upon Him in bodily form like a dove." Clearly this was an upon relationship with the Holy Spirit, a total immersion with the Spirit, supplying the power to launch Jesus into powerful, effective service. Through this experience, the Father was empowering his Son to move into three years' public ministry, the like of which has never been witnessed in all history.

It is interesting to note from *John 3:34* that God did not give Jesus his Spirit sparingly. The Bible uses the words: "To Him God gives the Spirit without limit." So Jesus did have a different filling from us. From the outset his filling was perfect, complete and continuous, but also without measure or limitation. This was *pleres* filling, in contrast to an often-repeated filling within us.

When did this begin?

I believe that, as with John, it began before his birth. If you disagree and say that Jesus was filled only at the age of 30 years, you have serious theological questions to answer. How is it possible that Jesus, who like us was perfectly human, could be left to live the perfect life demanded of Him in order to be our Saviour, without the help of the Holy Spirit? Not one of all the millions of people born since Adam has managed to live a sinless life. We have God's Word for this in *Romans 3:23*: "For all have sinned and come short of the glory of God."

We ourselves know that we fail constantly, until at last we have to admit our failure before God. There is no victory until we ask Him to take over our life, to fill us with his Holy Spirit, and to control us. We have to admit that we cannot change ourselves, but that God alone can make us more and more like Jesus.

Jesus, filled with the Holy Spirit

In the light of the perfect, complete, continuous filling apportioned without measure to Jesus, the picture appears to be as follows:

From the time the Holy Spirit overshadowed Mary, He never left the growing babe. He kept Him free from the sin inherent in Mary. After his birth, the Holy Spirit was the controlling power in his life, filling Him within his Spirit. Control came through the Spirit to the brain, and from there to all the parts of the body.

Never did an unseemly word pass those lips, never was a selfish thought entertained in that mind. There was never a time, even as a teenager, that He was ever disobedient to his parents, as is clear from *Luke 2:51*: (Jesus) "Went down to Nazareth with them and was obedient to them."

Nor did he ever speak a strong word to his brothers. Later, when He was a carpenter, there was never any disagreement with his customers. Though He was tempted in all points as we are, He never sinned, but was truly filled and controlled by the Holy Spirit in his human nature (*Heb 4:15*). The difference between Jesus and us is that Jesus had a mind constantly in tune with God. Our minds must still be renewed as we allow the Word of God to change our thinking.

The point in stressing the filling of the Holy Spirit in Jesus' life is that his life was made perfect through the Holy Spirit's inward power. Jesus' life is a pattern for ours. If it was necessary for Him to be filled, how much more necessary is it for us, for this aspect of the Holy Spirit's work has to do with the way we live.

Jesus' perfect filling led to his perfect life. Though our lives on earth will never be as perfect, we shall never change without the filling power of the Holy Spirit.

How does this filling apply to us?

We can experience interruptions in our filling with the Spirit. The devil sometimes catches us off guard, and before we know it, we have used unkind words or entertained evil thoughts. Thank God, we have the precious blood of Jesus to wash away our sins as we submit and confess them immediately to the Lord. In this way we can maintain our filling with the Holy Spirit by faith.

The word *plerousthe* used for the word "filled" in *Ephesians 5:18:* "Be ye filled with the Holy Spirit", is in the present tense, imperative mood, and passive voice. The present tense suggests a continuous experience, and we are responsible not to fill our minds with unclean thoughts. This is an act of the will. It presupposes that we shall lose the filling if we allow sin in. The blood of Jesus is available to wash us clean so that we may be constantly filled anew with the Holy Spirit.

The imperative mood means that God gives us no option. It is a command. We cannot say, "Well, my work is at such a stage that I have to put it first." One's work then becomes an idol. In fact, anything can become an idol. For the children of Israel it was a calf. For us, it might be our car, or a girlfriend or a boyfriend. The Israelites made an idol of the things of Egypt and longed for them. For us the things of Egypt might be the world. Anything that takes the place of God is an idol, and, if one is filled with self, one cannot be filled with the Holy Spirit. The big "I" is the worst idol of all.

The passive voice means we need not strive to be filled with the Spirit. This is something which God does for us. We must yield ourselves like clay in the hands of the potter. Yielding and faith are the essential ingredients. We have to trust God and then be bold enough to acknowledge this. "Thank you, Lord, you have filled me with your Holy Spirit," is the positive declaration we should be making.

Can we have the *pleres* type of filling like Jesus had? *Acts 7:55* says of Stephen before his martyrdom that he was "pleres" filled as he "looked up to heaven, and saw the glory of God, and Jesus standing at the right hand of God." Stephen seemed not to notice the battering stones thumping him to death. He saw Jesus. He said, "Lord, do not hold this sin against them". He fell asleep with the *pleres* filling. All self had gone – only Jesus remained. So to have the *pleres* filling is possible for us as it was with Stephen. God's word confirms this in *Ephesians 4:13*: "Attaining to the whole measure of the fullness of Christ."

Jesus baptised with the Holy Spirit

There can be no doubt that Jesus had a different and new experience of the Holy Spirit in Luke, Chapter 3. The experience He had then is called the baptism of the Holy Spirit; immersed with the Holy Spirit. *Luke 3:21–22* says: "Now when all the people were baptised, it came to pass that Jesus was baptised too. And as He was praying, heaven was opened and the Holy Spirit descended on Him in bodily form like a dove, and a voice came from heaven: 'You are My Son, whom I love; with you I am well pleased!'"

Whenever the baptism of the Holy Spirit is referred to in the Scriptures, the term "upon" is used. The Greek preposition *epi* should never be translated as "in". The picture here is that the Holy Spirit came down upon Jesus, immersing Jesus with Himself. From then on the enveloping power of the Holy Spirit never left Him. If we could have seen Jesus with spiritual eyes as Peter, James and John saw Him on the Mount of Transfiguration (*Mark 9:3*) we would have seen not only the traditional halo around his head, but that there was an enveloping light over all his person! This was the invisible "Light" of the Holy Spirit.

The empowering experience changed Jesus so dramatically that we should examine this in greater detail to see if there could be a similar change in store for us. We have already stressed the perfect, sinless life of our Lord Jesus, because He was filled with the Holy Spirit without limit.

There could be no change in this area of his life. During the first thirty years of his life, Jesus did not heal the sick nor did He do any miracle. He did not preach, nor did prophecy come from his lips; neither a "word of knowledge", nor a "word of wisdom". No supernatural power passed from Him when someone touched the hem of his garment, no evil spirits were discerned by Him, and none were cast out. It is clear that in Nazareth, where he probably spent 25 years of his life, the people saw nothing of this kind of ministry. Witness what we are told happened in *Mark 6:1–3* when He paid a return visit to his home: "Jesus left there and went to His home town accompanied by His disciples. When the Sabbath came, He began to teach in the synagogue, and many who heard Him were amazed. 'Where did this man get these things?' they asked: 'What's this wisdom that has been given to Him, that He even does miracles! Isn't this the carpenter? Isn't this Mary's son and the brother of James and Joses, Judas and Simon? Aren't His sisters here with us? "And they took offence at Him."

Luke 4:18 adds the fact that He read from the scroll of Isaiah (KJ): "The Spirit of the Lord is upon me, because He hath anointed me to preach the gospel to the poor; He hath sent me to heal the broken-hearted, to preach deliverance to the captives and recovery of sight to the blind, to set at liberty them that are bruised, to preach the acceptable year of the Lord."

Was it because of the baptism of the Holy Spirit upon Him that Jesus, the carpenter, was suddenly able to do all these things? Yes. In John's account of the baptism of Jesus, there is no doubt that the baptism or complete immersion of the Holy Spirit is meant.

John 1:32–33 reads: "John gave this testimony: 'I saw the Spirit come down from heaven as a dove, and remain on Him. The man on whom you see the Spirit come down and remain is He who will baptise you with the Holy Spirit.'" So Jesus had a continuous immersion of the Holy Spirit. This was not the initial experience of the filling which He had already had.

What about us?

If we ask the Lord Jesus, He will baptise us with the Holy Spirit, but in our case the power of the Holy Spirit is not "without measure" as it was with Jesus. *John 3:34* says: "To Jesus God gives the Holy Spirit without limit." We will receive the baptism with the Holy Spirit according to our submission, and according to the measure of our faith. Jesus' baptism was at 100 % power from the start.

Would any of us claim to have as much power now as Jesus did? Our goal is to arrive at the perfection of Jesus. Therefore, we must have a continuous growth in this "power" experience of the Holy Spirit. Do you agree? *Mark 6:4–5* (KJ) makes it clear that Jesus required a response of faith to perform His miracles: "And He could there do no mighty work, save that He laid His hand upon a few sick folk, and healed them."

Matthew adds, "And He marvelled because of their unbelief." *Luke 4:28–33* adds this sad ending: "And all they in the synagogue, when they heard these things, were filled with wrath, and rose up, and thrust Him out of the city, and led Him to the brow of the hill whereon their city was built, that they might throw Him down headlong. But He, passing through the midst of them, went His way, and came down to Capernaum, a city of Galilee, and taught them on the Sabbath days, and they were astonished at

His doctrine, for His words were with power."

Friends, do not despise the baptism in the Holy Spirit. Such an attitude is close to blasphemy, and not one of us would knowingly grieve the Holy Spirit, would we?

Jesus needed the baptism with the Holy Spirit. Do we?

We need the inward filling of the Holy Spirit to live the Christian life, and we need the immersion in the Holy Spirit to turn us into powerful witnesses. As we yield by faith we should be able to move into the gifts of the Holy Spirit, just as Jesus did. There may be hindrances blocking the Holy Spirit's free movement in our lives.

The need for inner healing of mind and emotions could be one of them. An inability to forgive others, or resentment and criticism certainly blocks the Holy Spirit. We need to yield ourselves more and more to Him, and be more willing to hear and obey his inner voice speaking to us. This will ensure a steady growth of the inner filling for a life of victory over sin, and a powerful outward baptism with the Holy Spirit for a fearless life of witness. Our witness is backed up by God's Word which is so powerful. God says in *Psalm 138:2* that his name and his Word are exalted above all things.

The thought of a growth in one's experience with the Holy Spirit might seem strange to some Christians – particularly those who have been taught otherwise:

1. Some have been taught that one is baptised with the Holy Spirit at conversion, whereas the Scripture teaches in *1 Corinthians 12:13* that: "We have all been baptised by the Holy Spirit into Christ's one body." All Christians throughout the world are part of Christ's body. Let us rejoice in this unifying fact. We are brothers and sisters in the Lord! This is the one baptism all Christians experience. Not everyone receives the baptism with the Holy Spirit and power for witness which is only given by Jesus Christ (*Luke 3:16; Acts 1:8*). This is the experience in which we should grow.

2. Others have been taught that the baptism in the Holy Spirit is an initial or first filling, never to be repeated. If this were true there could be no growth, because then the baptism is regarded as a once-for-all-time-experience. In answer to this, I can see that the devil would like you to believe this, so that you never move on to as great a baptism as Jesus had. God's Word settles the argument:

Ephesians 4:12–13 tells us "to prepare God's people for works of service, so that the body of Christ may be built up until we all reach unity in the faith and in the knowledge of the Son of God and become mature, attaining to the whole measure of the fullness of Christ."

1 Corinthians 2:4–5 says: "My message and my preaching were not with wise and persuasive words, but with a demonstration of the Spirit's power, so that your faith might not rest on men's wisdom, but on God's power."

I have no doubt that this is the picture that God wants us to see when we desire to be used by the Holy Spirit. Once this picture is clearly seen, there won't be so many people falling back into their former ways.

When Jesus returns to this earth for his reign of a thousand years, we with our spiritual bodies will be able to see the glory of the Holy Spirit still upon Him. After his resurrection, Jesus still worked *in the power of the Holy Spirit,* as we are told in *Acts 1:2:* "Until the day in which He was taken up to heaven, after giving instructions through the Holy Spirit to the apostles whom He had chosen".

What about us?

By now I am sure you have trusted Jesus for the baptism with the Holy Spirit. See yourself in the full potential of this experience: empowered through the Holy Spirit to live a life pleasing to God, plus a life of power where the gifts of the spirit are manifested in your life.

We must set ourselves the goal of moving ahead and experiencing a growth in this "twinfold" experience with the Holy Spirit. The late Pastor Ingidi, who was often used in the healing and miracle ministry in South Africa, did not just stumble on this ministry. God led him step by step, until by faith in the name of Jesus he was able to command the blind to see and they saw immediately.

Why is everyone who is baptised with God's Holy Spirit not able to do this? Because not everyone is willing to pay the price which growth involves. Every year during his month's holiday, Ingidi would withdraw to the mountains and spend that month waiting on the Lord in prayer. Most of us want to spend that time pursuing pleasure, enjoying a well-earned rest. We are unwilling to spend the time really getting to know our Heavenly Father and to hear what He wants to do for us.

Pastor Reinhard Bonnke, a man probably more used of God in the preaching ministry in the countries of Africa and other parts of the world than anyone else, has had up to half a million people in a single service. Stadiums are too small for the services and so a large piece of open ground has to be chosen. Thousands are born again in a single meeting. On a single command, thousands more are miraculously healed. It is almost as it was with Jesus.

Luke 7:22 tells us: "The blind receive their sight, the lame walk, ... the deaf hear, ... and the Good News is preached to the poor." His ministry is experiencing steady spiritual growth with Holy Spirit anointing and he is being used in more and greater miracles.

What is happening? A greater filling, producing the fruits of the Spirit, a greater baptism resulting in more power for preaching, as well as a fuller use of the gifts of the Holy Spirit. It is clear, beloved friends, from all this that God wants us to move on to greater things. Let us open our eyes to see what He is doing, especially as the time is short. Let us be willing and allow God to accelerate our progress into all that He wants to do for us.

Let us be willing to pay the price of dedication and obedience to his will, rather than be hindered by a narrow theology, let us have an on-going, expanding theology. Some of us haven't changed our theological ideas for 10 years or more! Theology, of course, must be based on God's Word, but let us update ourselves, let us not settle for what we think God's Word says. God's will for us is clear in *3 John: 2* (New Trans.): "My beloved, I desire that above all things you prosper and be in good health, even as your soul prospers."

To prosper means much more than to prosper financially. It means to become mature spiritually; it means to have a full, mature understanding of God's Word; it means to walk in good health. The soul refers to the mind, so it means to have a growing spiritual intellect controlled by the Holy Spirit. It means to have an abundance in all things so that you can give of yourself and enrich all whom you meet.

2 Corinthians 9:11–12 says: "You will be made rich in every way so that you can be generous on every occasion ... supplying the needs of God's people." Do you begin to feel the excitement of moving with the Lord? Jesus is truly coming soon, and much has to be done to make ourselves ready for the greatest spiritual revival the world has ever seen. This revival is already here. At the Hatfield Community in Pretoria our people have already seen its impact. Whatever God has planned for us we will move with it. This revival will be like no other. God never does the same thing more than once in exactly the same way.

He says in *Isaiah 42:9*: "See, the former things have taken place, and new things I declare; before they spring into being I announce them to you." If one turns the page to *Isaiah 43:19*, we hear God saying: "Forget the former things; do not dwell on the past. See, I am doing a new thing." When we flip over to the New Testament, God's word says in *Acts 13:41*: "I am going to do something in your days, that you would never believe, even if someone told you."

Numbers 23:19 encourages us to take hold of these promises of God and to believe for them for our generation now: "Does God speak and then not act? Does He promise and not fulfil?" God is waiting for those who will take hold of his promises as if they were meant for our day and re-declare them for our day, for they are meant for our day!

When revival comes to your church, don't reject it because it is not what you expect. God has already warned you it won't be something like you could imagine! The things which have happened in our church at Hatfield often have been unusual, but Pastor Ed together with all the other pastors, decided that the church would move with the Holy Spirit. If the devil tries to counterfeit something God is well able to give discernment whether something is from Him or not. The Hatfield Christian Church was birthed in the charismatic revival and grew to more than 6 000. We have been in the end time revival for two years already and believe we are still only in the fringe of it.

What has characterised this revival is that God Himself has counselled people. Suddenly people have fallen out of their chairs and are seen lying on the carpet totally unaware of anyone else around them. When you speak to them afterwards they tell you amazing stories of how God spoke to them in words and visions. This exactly met their need. Others have begun to laugh or cry, seemingly out of control as this has sometimes gone on for hours.

These people have received emotional healing that no amount of human counselling could achieve. If people become a disturbance to the worship, the deacons merely carry them out to the chapel next to the main auditorium. The solution is simple! We have trusted God in the situation and in no way will we retract the freedom God has to do what He wants. The revival is his.

You say, yes, I see! I want to have the Holy Spirit filling my life, enabling me to mature in all the fruits of the Spirit. I want the Lord Jesus to baptise me with His Holy Spirit. I want to move into his supernatural miracle-working gifts, as He sees fit to impart them to me.

How do I do it? By faith. Never try to be better, for you will never feel worthy. Exercise faith, and Jesus will see to all the rest. *Galatians 3:3* (KJ) asks: "Receive ye the Holy Spirit by the works of he law, or by the hearing of faith?" and *Galatians 3:5*: "He therefore that ministereth to you the Spirit, and worketh miracles among you, doeth he it by the Works of the law or by the hearing of faith?"

Galatians 3:14 says: "That the blessings of Abraham might come on the Gentiles (that is, the receiving of Christ by faith) through Jesus Christ; that we all might receive the realisation of the promise of the Holy Spirit (in His manifold aspects) by faith."

Let this be our prayer: "Lord Jesus, thank you for making it your responsibility to baptise your children with your Holy Spirit. Do this to me now. Just as I received You into my heart by faith, I now trust You to fill me and baptise me with your Holy Spirit. Change me, and make me willing to move into all your gifts now. Thank you, Lord Jesus. Amen."

The baptism with the Holy Spirit, a "twin-fold" experience

9

Some of you experience difficulty in receiving some of the teaching on the Holy Spirit even though it is strictly word based. After writing this last chapter I had a remarkable experience which confirmed this teaching on the baptism with the Holy Spirit. It happened this way:

At 01:45 one Sunday morning in November I awoke to hear Jesus speaking to me. It was so clear, I at first thought it was audible. Then I realised that the words were coming from inside of me. I thought then if I opened my eyes I was going to see Jesus sitting next to me. I did, but to my amazement all I saw was the darkness of night! I felt a little disappointed, but was encouraged because as soon as I closed my eyes there was this voice again with its clear, rich tones.

My memory became very clear. Jesus spoke to me for 45 minutes. He finished: "You can now go and preach this sermon without notes." I did preach it four times that very day in the prison ministry. I serve the Lord in seven prisons in our rainbow nation. The blacks have given me a nickname, 'Thandabantu', which means someone who loves the people. This I can thank God for as it is the Holy Spirit shedding abroad God's love in my heart.

Then Jesus said, "I want you to get up and write this all out as a permanent record." I got up at 2:45 and wrote all the way through to 6:30. I wasn't a bit tired because of the energising flow of the Holy Spirit.

Jesus then said to me: "This is how I got my sermons. When I withdrew to pray, a good deal of that time my Father taught Me, and brought all the messages I preached to my conscious mind. He did it through the Holy Spirit living in Me." Jesus said again, "You have been asking Me exactly what meditation is all about? What you have experienced this morning is true meditation."

To explain this fully I must add that everything Jesus said to me in thoughts to my mind, I repeated to myself in a whisper. I then found out that the Hebrew word for meditate is, to say it over to yourself! Don't hesitate to ask the Holy Spirit what certain scriptures mean.

These are the things Jesus said to me:

"I want all my children to be clothed with power from above"

Jesus said: "Too many of My children are satisfied with a small deposit of the Holy Spirit, when I want them to be flooded with Him." He then quoted 2 *Corinthians* to me, *1:21–22* in the New International Version: "He anointed us, set His seal of ownership on us, and put His Spirit in our hearts as a deposit, guaranteeing what is to come." It interested me greatly that Jesus sounded modern enough not to use the King James! He said: "There is so much the Holy Spirit wants to do for My children, but they limit the Holy Spirit by being satisfied with a small deposit within the inner man. I want them to trust me for the guarantee of what is to come." Then Jesus took me to *Luke 24:49*: "I am going to send you what My Father has promised; but stay in the city until you have been clothed with power from on high."

He explained: "This is the guarantee of what is to come. The working of the Holy Spirit in ever increasing measure in the lives of My children. This word 'clothed' appears only once in the New Testament and is very rich in meaning. It was chosen especially to explain the full work of the Holy Spirit. The Greek word is *enduo.* It means to clothe, but much more: the Greeks used it to invest a king with his kingly robe and crown of authority and power. His whole person was enveloped to the floor with this beautiful robe. This is a picture of what the Holy Spirit wants to do for us."

Jesus continued. "It means much more than to be clothed with authority and power. It means to be filled throughout your whole person with the Holy Spirit." Jesus used a sponge as an illustration. He said: "Imagine you are sitting in a bath of water. If you take a sponge and soak it in the water, what happens to it?" I replied that it gets fully saturated with the water. "Precisely", said Jesus. "I want all my children to be so filled with the Holy Spirit as to be saturated with Him. When you hold a sponge up out of the water, the water runs from it. My children should have this living water flow from them to others, especially when squeezed or persecuted."

Jesus said to me: "Everything I ever did on earth was done in dependence on the Holy Spirit. Even after I rose from the dead, and even now I depend on the Holy Spirit." He then quoted *Acts 1:2*: "He gave instructions through the Holy Spirit to the apostles He had chosen." "How much more should My children depend on the Holy Spirit!"

I asked how we could avail ourselves of this energising power of the Holy Spirit, and Jesus replied: "By yielding fully to the Holy Spirit's control and by launching out in faith and dependence upon Him. You see, Jack," He said, "the experience of the Baptism with the Holy Spirit is a 'twinfold' experience – both a clothing with power and authority to have a fruitful ministry in the gifts of the Holy Spirit, and a saturation within to show forth a pleasing Christian life with a full manifestation of the fruits of the spirit."

The baptism is a "twinfold" experience

I already saw perfectly what Jesus was saying. The first thing I did when I got up was to check out in Strong's concordance if the word *enduo* only appeared once. This was proof to me that Jesus was truly speaking to me. I then looked up Thayer's Greek Lexicon. This is what it says on the word *enduo*: To envelop in, to hide in, to clothe with a garment, to protect with armour, to be adorned with power. To have a new purpose in life, to become so saturated with the mind of Christ, in thought, feeling and action as to resemble Him, to reproduce the life He lived.

I can hear you saying with me, "This is what I want." This is what our Father promised, so let us receive all this by faith.

Jesus stressed that this is his command, that his children be baptised with the Holy Spirit (*Acts 1:4–5*). He said that He Himself did not commence ministry until He had been baptised with the Holy Spirit. There is an inward power, which enables one to break free from sin and live a life that pleases God. Then there is an outward power (*Acts 1:8*) which is the "being clothed with" aspect of the Holy Spirit. This gives us power for service and can be used in the gifts of the Holy Spirit.

Jesus went on to say: "I am preparing my church for the greatest outpouring of the Holy Spirit that the world has ever seen. I want those of you who have missed the charismatic revival up to now to put away the doctrinal thoughts that have kept you from the full power of my blessing. I commend many of you for believing that the inward work of the Holy Spirit will give you victory over sin. Now I say in this end-time, this is not enough in order to be a recruit in my end-time army and harvest people for the Kingdom of God. To you who have been used in the gifts, I will not condone a sinful and uncontrolled life. Repent, as your lives have brought shame to my body."

Jesus further declared: "Strife and argument shall cease in My Church for I have declared that they shall be one, so that the whole world may know that My Father did send me (John 17:23). My Father gave Me to the world and I accepted willingly so that all who believe will receive eternal life. I am now calling those who will dedicate themselves to intercession in prayer, to make this oneness a reality. I have made the work of intercession easy, for the best way to intercede is in tongues. These words are the wisdom of the Holy Spirit and He is in complete accord with what the Father and Son want to accomplish. I command you, write the vision down and publish it so that My Church may run with it."

I have no doubt that this message is the truth about the Holy Spirit. Jesus confirmed it to me personally. Then shortly after this experience I had another beautiful confirmation. Ivy, my wife, and I are covenant partners with Kenneth and Gloria Copeland. This is what brother Kenneth wrote in one of his *Voice of Victory* magazines which confirms this "twinfold" experience of the Holy Spirit:

"The Spirit of God within you produces nine fruits. The Spirit of God upon you by the anointing of God, produces nine gifts for service. The nine fruits are for character and power in your inward spiritual life and holiness. The nine gifts of the Spirit are all to be used to minister to and help others."

I believe that statement is inspired by the Holy Spirit and could not be a better summary of the doctrine of the Holy Spirit. This is what God's end-time church needs. Brothers and sisters in the Lord, let us cultivate the love, fellowship and help of the Holy Spirit in our lives, to experience the full measure of his power.

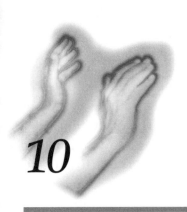

The personality of the Holy Spirit

10

It is of the utmost importance in the Christian life to understand the Holy Spirit as a Person. To regard Him as an influence or a power emanating from God is grave error. Some have even prayed for power as if God would entrust them with his power.

Thinking along such lines can lead to the misconception that man is able to use God's power. We pray "Thine is the kingdom, the power and the glory" and this is right. Even as God's children we cannot use God's power as if we only have to flick a switch. The Holy Spirit does powerful things through us if we allow Him to reside in us. That is why God has the glory.

The kind of prayer that God can answer indicates a willingness to yield and a longing to be used by the Holy Spirit. If we have a desire to yield, then we could pray: "Father, on the basis of what Your Son has done for me, fill me with Your Holy Spirit, and use me as your channel to accomplish your will."

The Holy Spirit will not force Himself on anyone, but if we yield to his will He can begin to work through us. The thought then is: "How can He have more of us?" We will be in subjection to a Higher Person who is infinitely holy, infinitely wise, infinitely mighty, yet tender. We will never get to know an "influence", but we will get to know the Holy Spirit as a Person.

How is He to be known as a person?

Naturally, we must not think of Him as a person with a body. That He has no body is a distinct advantage, as He can indwell the spirit and heart of every believer and we can know Him in the following ways:

1. A person has the power of thought and knowledge. *1 Corinthians 2:10–11*: "No mind has conceived what God has prepared for those who love Him, But God has revealed it to us by His Spirit; for the Holy Spirit searches all things, even the deep things of God. For who among men knows the thoughts of a man except man's spirit within him? In the same way no one knows the thoughts of God except the Spirit of God." The Holy Spirit is a Divine Being who has all the Father's knowledge. He lives in our spirits and He communicates through this inward knowing, which *Romans 8:16* calls the Holy Spirit witnessing with our spirit.

2. A person has the power of choice and of free will. *1 Corinthians 12:11*: "All these are the work of one and the same Spirit, and He gives His gifts to each man just as He determines."

3. The Spirit is infallible, and He has an infinite mind. *Romans 8:27*: "And He (the Father) searches our hearts, knows the mind of the Spirit." From the mind emanates thought, feeling and purpose. Only a person can have these attributes.

4. The Spirit has infinite love. *Romans 15:30*: "By our Lord Jesus Christ and by the love of the Holy Spirit, to join me in my struggle by praying to God for me." We can also say "the Spirit's love sought me out and finally brought me to Jesus Christ," can't we?

5. The Spirit can be grieved. *Ephesians 4:30*: "Do not grieve the Holy Spirit of God, with whom you were sealed for the day of redemption."

He is utterly holy and no part of Him has any suggestion of sin. If we drop down to the level of sin, we grieve Him, and we have to apologise and ask for the cleansing power of the blood of Jesus, for He cannot use a partially clean vessel.

What the Holy Spirit does

Only a person can do what is ascribed to the Holy Spirit:

1. He speaks. When God speaks, He speaks by his Holy Spirit. *Revelation 2:7*: "He who has an ear, let him hear what the Spirit says to the churches"; *1 Corinthians 2:1*: "But God has revealed them unto us by His Spirit"; *Romans 8:16*: "The Holy Spirit Himself witnesses with our spirit that we are children of God" (that is, He speaks into our spirits).

2. He teaches. *John 14:26*: "But the Comforter who is the Holy Spirit ... He will teach you all things."

3. He guides. *John 16:13*: "But when the Spirit of truth is come, He will guide you into all truth."

4. He shows you the future and glorifies Jesus. *John 16:13–14*: "He will not speak on His own, He will speak only what He hears from the Father. He will tell you what is yet to come." The things God has prepared for us, not only in heaven but also what He has in store for us here, God reveals to us through his Spirit speaking to our spirits. *1 Corinthians 2:10* quoted above is an affirmation of this work of the Holy Spirit.

5. He leads and commands with authority. *Romans 8:14*: "Those who are led by the Spirit of God, are the Sons of God"; *Acts 16:6* (KJ): "Now when they had gone through Phrygia and all the regions of Galatia, they were forbidden of the Holy Spirit to preach the Word in Asia"; *Acts 13:2*: "As they ministered to the Lord and fasted, the Holy Spirit said, 'Separate Me Barnabas and Paul for the work whereunto I have called them'."

The Spirit has taken the place of Jesus on earth

John 16:7 (KJ) says: "Nevertheless I tell you the truth. It is expedient for you that I go away, for if I go not away, the Comforter will not come to you, but if I depart I will send Him to you." *John 14:16* tells us: "And I will pray the Father and He shall give you another Comforter (of the same kind) that He might abide with you forever." Still further, *1 John 3:24* says: "And hereby we know that Jesus abides in us by the Holy Spirit He has given us."

The Holy Spirit has come back as Jesus' other self, another of the same kind. He is not limited by a body, and so can enter the heart or spirit of every believer. We should from this moment hear his voice. Finally, we have to understand that the Holy Spirit is such a holy Person that no word should ever be spoken against Him. *Matthew 12:31–32* (KJ) reads: "Wherefore I say unto you, all manner of sin and blasphemy shall be forgiven unto men; but the blasphemy against the Holy Spirit shall not be forgiven unto men. And whosoever speaketh a word against the Son of Man, it shall be forgiven him; but whosoever speaketh against the Holy Spirit, it shall not be forgiven him, neither in this world, neither in the world to come."

Such is the seriousness of disregarding the Person of the Holy Spirit. You cannot blaspheme against a thing, an influence or anything impersonal. You can only blaspheme against a person.

He is worthy of our love and confidence as He is Jesus' other self. 'God, too, was in Christ, reconciling the world to Himself.' How was this done? By the Holy Spirit, the third Person in the Trinity (*Luke 3:21–22*). The Father spoke from heaven, Jesus was on earth and the Holy Spirit came down upon Jesus. The Spirit is our Comforter and Friend. We need Him, and He needs us. He needs our human lips to speak through. He needs holy lives to work through. Will you let Him apply the blood of Jesus to make you a clean vessel?

Not only is the Holy Spirit a person, but He is God. Do you remember the story of Ananias and Sapphira, his wife? I want to quote an exerpt from that story. *Acts 5:3–4:* "Then Peter said, 'Ananias, how is it that Satan has so filled your heart that you have lied to the Holy Spirit ... You have not lied to men but to God.'" Here we are clearly told that the Holy Spirit is God. With what respect the Christian should regard the Holy Spirit! We have God living inside us. He is our Comforter, Counsellor, Helper, Intercessor, Advocate, Strengthener, Standby, Enabler, Upholder, Empowerer, Ability giver, Teacher, Protector and Guide. Let us allow Him to do his work in us. We need a Person who can do all this in us and He does not charge for his services!

The importance of the Baptism with the Holy Spirit in the early church

11

The baptism with the Holy Spirit was foremost in the thinking of the early church

Acts 8:14–17 says: "When the apostles in Jerusalem heard that Samaria had accepted the Word of God, they sent Peter and John to them. When they arrived they prayed for them that they might receive the Holy Spirit, because the Holy Spirit had not yet come upon any of them; they had simply been baptised in the name of the Lord Jesus. Then Peter and John laid their hands on them and they received the Holy Spirit."

Does this mean that if you have received Christ you possibly may not have the Holy Spirit? The answer is no. It is not possible to receive Christ without having the Holy Spirit. The following points will explain why this is so.

Many Christians go wrong in their understanding of these verses in *Acts 8*. Our theology must be clear. Many Bible colleges teach that you must take your doctrine only from the Epistles. If this were so, Acts is excluded from theology. This is an erroneous view, for "the Scripture cannot be broken" *(John 10:35)*. The way to get a clear picture in theology is to compare scripture with scripture, not a part, but the whole.

What you picture in your theology is what you are going to believe. If your picture is wrong, your theology will be wrong. It is also a fallacy to believe that the apostles could make no mistakes, and that they had a perfect theology. Certainly at this stage Peter and John did not have a complete theology. Peter still believed that the Gospel was only for the Jews. He still did not believe his own sermon at Pentecost. In his sermon he quoted the Old Testament, saying "The Father's promise of the Holy Spirit is unto you and your children and to all that are afar off, even as many as the Lord our God shall call" *(Acts 2:39)*. "Afar off" implies other countries as well. Peter was reluctant to take the Gospel to the Gentiles and God had to put great pressure on him to go to the house of Cornelius in Acts, Chapter 10.

Why am I saying this? Because many have the theologically defective view that receiving the Holy Spirit is synonymous with being baptised with the Holy Spirit. This view is inferred from *Acts 8:17*, regarding the Samaritan Christians. "Peter and John placed their hands on them and they received the Holy Spirit." We tend to forget that verse 16 says: "The Holy Spirit had not yet come upon any of them." The "upon" relationship is the baptism of the Holy Spirit, that is, his power for service, as in *Acts 1:8*. So Peter and John laid their hands on them for power in service and the manifestation of the gifts of the Spirit.

A person cannot base doctrine on one or two scriptures. You have to find out what the Bible teaches as a whole. The fact is that the Holy Spirit was already living in the hearts of these Samaritan believers. What happened was that the Holy Spirit came upon them in the baptism for power and enabled them to move into the precious gifts of the Spirit.

What is the authority for making such statements as these? The Bible!

If Jesus is your Saviour, do you have the Holy Spirit within you?

The answer is yes, if you have confessed that Jesus Christ is your Lord. When we compare scriptures, it becomes abundantly clear that every Christian has the precious Holy Spirit living within. Consider just these few passages: *Ephesians 1:13–14* (LB): "Because of what Christ did, and your trust in Him, you are marked as belonging to Him, by the Holy Spirit. His presence within us is God's guarantee of the Spirit's seal that God has purchased us and guarantees to bring us to Himself."

1 John 3:24 (KJ): "And hereby we know that he – Jesus – lives in us by the Holy Spirit He has given us." The moment we receive Christ as Saviour into our hearts the Holy Spirit comes in.

Romans 8:9: "If anyone does not have the Spirit of Christ he does not belong to Christ."

Of course, the Spirit of Christ here is identical with the Holy Spirit. There can be no fourth Person in the Trinity.

2 Corinthians 1:22: "God has set His seal of ownership on us and put the Spirit in our hearts as a deposit, guaranteeing what is to come."

2 Corinthians 5:17 (New Trans.): "If anyone is in Christ he is created anew inside, the old has gone, a new life has begun."

It is the Holy Spirit that creates the new spirit in us. He lives in this new spirit, which is sometimes called the heart.

Romans 8:16: "The Spirit testifies within our spirit that we are children of God."

1 John 2:27 (LB): "But you have the Holy Spirit and He lives within you, in your hearts, so you don't need anyone to teach you what is right. For the Holy Spirit teaches you all things and He is the TRUTH and no liar."

Beloved fellow Christians, we must learn to rely on the Holy Spirit. He first testifies with our spirits that we are children of God, the most important thing in the Christian life. The Scriptures here declare that the Holy Spirit can be relied upon to teach us.

1 John 4:13: "We know that we live in Him and He is in us, because He has given us of His Spirit."

1 John 5:6 (LB): "We know that God exists and is real. The Holy Spirit, forever truthful, says it. So we have three witnesses, the voice of the Holy Spirit in our hearts, the voice of heaven at Christ's baptism and the voice before He died."

1 Peter 1:2 (LB): "The Father chose you long ago, knowing you would become His children and the Holy Spirit has been at work in your hearts, cleansing you with the blood of Jesus."

1 Corinthians 2:12: "We have not received the spirit of the world, but the Spirit who is from God, that we may understand what God has freely given us."

1 Corinthians 2:14: "The man without the Spirit does not accept the things that come from the Spirit of God, for they are foolishness to him."

1 Corinthians 3:16: "Don't you know that you yourselves are God's temple and that God's Spirit lives in you?"

1 Corinthians 6:19: "Do you not know that your body is a temple of the Holy Spirit, who is in you, whom you have received from God?"

1 John 4:13 (LB): "And He has put His own Holy Spirit into our hearts as a proof to us that we are living in Him and He in us."

Here are fifteen scriptures which give us the assurance that, when we have given our lives to Jesus, we have the Holy Spirit within us. This is despite the fact that we receive nothing automatically in the Christian life. *James 4:2* says: "We have not, because we ask not." We have the Holy Spirit living within us by virtue of the fact that we asked our Saviour Jesus Christ to live within our hearts. The Christian is one who has responded to what Jesus said in *Revelation 3:20*: "Behold, I stand at the door (of our hearts) and knock. If any man hear My voice and open the door, I will come into him." *1 John 3:24* confirms: "We know that He (Jesus) lives in us. We know it by the Holy Spirit He gave us."

That settles it. You do have the Holy Spirit living in you! He will never leave you!

Does this mean that you are automatically filled?

The fact that the Christian has the Holy Spirit living in him does not mean that he or she is automatically filled and baptised with the Holy Spirit. We only get what we ask for, and what we allow.

We can ask with our lips and still debar the Holy Spirit from taking control of our lives. The inward control of the Holy Spirit is the filling. That is why yielding and obedience are so important. The opposite is to run our lives our way, at home, at work, at play.

God does not want to take anything away from us. He wants to be given a place, the first place in our lives. Tradition often takes precedence over what the Word of God says. For example, when we hear about or are invited to a charismatic service, our immediate reaction is "No, I've got my church." If we are critical of the Gifts of the Holy Spirit, we will certainly not receive the baptism with the Holy Spirit until we yield and acknowledge that God is right.

Friends, we can rely completely on the Holy Spirit. Let us not be critical of Him. *1 Thessalonians 5:19* says, "Quench not the Holy Spirit ", or, as it might be rendered, "Hinder not the Holy Spirit". This is very important, since the next verse says, "Despise not prophesyings." Prophecy is one of the Gifts of the Holy Spirit, and it is not to be despised. Verse 21 continues: "Test all things, hold fast that which is good." The body of believers should "test all things" and hold nothing that is contrary to God's Word.

Now we come back to our text in *Acts 8:15*. When Peter and John arrived in Samaria, they prayed that the believers "might receive the Holy Spirit." Does this mean that the 15 verses we have considered together are wrong? No, they simply complete the picture of the Holy Spirit's working. The clue is in the next verse, 16: "because the Holy Spirit had not yet come upon any of them." This refers to the complete experience of the Holy Spirit. The experience of being baptised with the Holy Spirit.

What is the baptism?

The "upon" relationship of the Holy Spirit is the baptism, the immersion of the believer by the Holy Spirit, which gives him power to witness for Jesus and to take authority over the enemy.

Obviously, in Samaria there was no evidence of the baptism of the Holy

Spirit, although in *Acts 10:44* it was evident in the house of Cornelius. "While Peter was still speaking these words, the Holy Spirit came on all them who heard the message." And verse 46: "For they heard them speaking in tongues and praising God."

Verse 45 says: "The circumcised believers who had gone with Peter were astonished that the gift of the Holy Spirit had been poured out even on the Gentiles." To them there was no doubt about the baptism. Why? Because there was an outward sign which could be seen and heard. They were using one of the gifts of the Holy Spirit, namely, the prayer and praise language. You will note that the word "gift" is used here. This has led many to believe that, since the words "gift", "filling" and "baptism" are used as if they are interchangeable, they are in fact interchangeable. This is to lose sight of the fact of verbal inspiration of God's word. If you contend that it does not matter what the meaning of a word in the original Greek or Hebrew is, and that you can make it mean what you want it to mean, then the Word of God loses much of its authority.

What happened in the house of Cornelius is similar to the experience at Pentecost when three things were evident: the gift of the Holy Spirit, the filling of the Holy Spirit, and the baptism of the Holy Spirit.

Though these Gentiles loved God, they were not yet Christians in the New Testament sense of the word, as they did not have the Holy Spirit living within. This only happened while Peter was preaching to them.

They received the full experience of the Holy Spirit as the people had at Pentecost. You don't necessarily receive the three aspects above automatically. It depends on what you trust God for. If you receive Jesus into your heart you receive the Holy Spirit as God's gift. If you don't believe in what the Bible calls the baptism and you only believe in the filling, you will only receive the filling. If you believe in all three and want power to witness for Christ you will be baptised with the Holy Spirit. You see, if you ask for bread you get bread and not a stone!

The word baptism is never used in this study to mean an initiation ceremony. Its correct meaning is immersion. Peter and John were sent to Samaria to make sure that the new converts there were baptised with the Holy Spirit. The gift of the Spirit was not enough; they had to have power to witness. The early church saw to it that these new converts moved into the power relationship of the Holy Spirit.

If the reader finds any confusion as to these three aspects of the Holy Spirit, turn back to the illustration on page 42.

We make a big mistake if we appoint Sunday School teachers or Christians to do any work for the Lord before they have been baptised with the Holy Spirit. No Christian need be without this experience. It is given by faith, and there is no necessity to wait for it. The Holy Spirit came nearly 2 000 years ago. He is here, to be received by faith in his filling and baptising power.

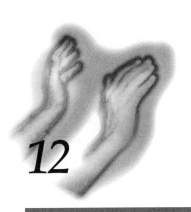

Hindrances to the Baptism

12

It could be unforgiveness or resentment

If you have not had this experience by faith, there must be some blockage. Ask the Lord what it is. It could be a lack of forgiveness or resentment against someone for something which happened years ago and which you have forgotten about. Perhaps someone wronged you, and you felt bruised inside.

Extend forgiveness and ask the Lord Jesus to heal the inner bruising. Unless you break the fetters created by an unforgiving spirit, the enemy will readily enmesh you for his next attack. The enemy has no mercy. He will "steal, kill and destroy" (*John 10:10*). Jesus wants to give you life, and give it abundantly. You can't have this more abundant life while you continue to give a foothold to the enemy.

Doubt could be one of the blockages

Mark 11:23 (New Trans.) says, "For truly I say unto you, that whosoever shall say to this mountain (blockage) be removed and be cast into the sea, and shall not doubt in his mind, but shall believe that the things he has confessed with his mouth will come to pass, he shall have whatever he says." Other translations use the words "Doubt in the heart." The word heart does not always refer to the spirit. It often refers to purely the mind, which is in the area of the soul, not the spirit where your faith comes from! When our Bibles use the word heart you have to judge from the context as to whether mind or spirit is meant.

If you say, "I don't know why I have not received the baptism with the Holy Spirit?", you see you are still in doubt. Modify what you say with *Mark 1:23*, and refuse to doubt in your heart which here is the mind. It will help you to realise that doubt comes from the area of the mind only and is not a product of the "born again" spirit. Jesus said this in *Luke 24:38* when He appeared to the disciples, and said: "Why are you troubled, and why do doubts rise in your minds?" Now we know doubts are always just from the mind and actually do not effect our faith, as faith comes from our spirit. *Romans 10:10* declares this to us strongly: "For it is with your heart you believe and are justified, and it's with your mouth that you confess and are saved." Here the word heart refers to our spirit.

Once you know this, you can keep your faith steady in the hardest of battles, while doubts assail your mind! How? You will say, "Jesus told me where doubts come from. They come from my mind." So with doubts attacking the mind you will say, "I believe from my spirit what the word of God says in *Luke 3:16*, 'He (Jesus) will baptise you with the Holy Spirit and with fire.' The word of God says Jesus will do it for me. Thank you Jesus, I believe you have baptised me with the Holy Spirit and with fire."

Like doubts, inner hurts or bruises come from the soul and not from the spirit.

Bruises of the soul, not the spirit

Unhealed bruises can also hinder the baptism from taking place, blocking faith. Satan regards these bruises, psychological and emotional, as part of his property. Jesus is the only one who can heal these wounds. We have to come to our Jesus and ask Him to heal us of every inner hurt He can see. Believe that He has done it and thank Him, for He came for this purpose. *Luke 4:18* (KJ) tells us: "The Spirit of the Lord is upon me ... to heal the broken-hearted, to give deliverance to the captives, and to set at liberty those who are bruised."

You feel this inner bruising inside your person, from your spirit. You might even say your spirit is hurting so bad inside and you just can't get rid of it. There is good news on the way. There is a way of deliverance. The bruising is actually not from your spirit, which is the eternal life of God in you, it is from the soul. Both feel inside! Your spirit is the born-again part, totally made new with nothing left of the old. The soul, however, is not born-again and comprises the mind, emotions, the inner feelings we have and our ability of free choice. We dare not let the part of us which is not born again dominate over the life of God in us, our spirits.

My wife Ivy was broken-hearted when our lovely granddaughter of nine, Tarynne, and her mother Robynne were tragically killed in a motor accident. Keegan and my son miraculously survived. It was a very hard time for the family. Fortunately both Robynne and Tarynne loved the Lord so we know that, "Absent from the body, they were present with the Lord."

Ivy and I were sitting together in church when Pastor Ed referred to *Isaiah 61:1*: "He has sent Me to bind up the broken-hearted." Jesus spoke to Ivy through this Scripture and then inside her heart said to her: "If you don't give me your broken heart how can I heal it?" Right then and there Ivy gave Jesus her broken heart and the healing began to take place inside from that moment. Now she can think briefly of the tragic event without feeling that terrible bruising inside. The broken heart here does not refer to the spirit part of our being, but to the soul. Jesus was "sent to bind up the broken-hearted."

Whatever caused the bruising, Jesus can heal it if you give the incident over to Him.

How do I get rid of these hindrances?

By confessing them to God.

Make this positive confession after me, say it out aloud and write the date in the margin as a witness that you have made this confession:

"I place all blockages of doubt, resentment, unforgiveness, harshness towards others, criticism and my judicial attitude beneath the blood of Jesus. Also my tendency to depreciate and belittle myself and others, all discord, jealousy, ambition, fits of depression and anger, every idol that means a lot to me and is a hindrance to my giving myself fully to You, my Lord and my God.

"All envy, unholy desires of sex outside of marriage, lack of self-control, fears of all kinds, all boastful attitudes, disobedience and lack of love. All excess of food and drink, and all immoral thoughts. Every time I have read a star guide, worn a lucky charm, put faith in a birthstone, had my fortune told or taken any part in the occult. These things I sincerely repent of and ask forgiveness for, and desire the washing of the precious blood of my Saviour Jesus Christ.

"I fully realise that in all these things I have given a foothold to the devil. On the ground that I know that Jesus purchased me with his precious blood, in the power of the Holy Spirit, I reclaim all the ground that I have ever given to the enemy.

"I repent of all this, my Father, and ask your forgiveness in Jesus' name. In order to receive your full, unreserved forgiveness, I extend forgiveness from a heart of love to everyone I must forgive, even if some of them are no longer living. There are cases where I was not to blame, where I was 99 % right and only 1 % wrong, but I take the lead and ask forgiveness. Where the person is still alive, give me the grace, Lord, to go to him and ask personal forgiveness without any self-justification.

"With all the authority of Jesus' name, I now command and, in fact, demand that every evil spirit that ever attacked me and brought me under bondage be gone, for I expel them from me.

"Further, I use the key given to me by Jesus, my Saviour and Deliverer, in Matthew 16:19 and bind every one of these evil spirits and command them to remain in a desert place until Jesus Christ returns to the earth. Father, You also said whatever I release on earth will be released in heaven. I now release myself into Your care and declare myself to be free of all bondage of the enemy, the devil, in the Name of Jesus. Thank you, Father, for making all this a reality to me."

Another hindrance: not setting a time or place for receiving the baptism

A friend of mine put all this into practice, but still did not receive the baptism of God's Holy Spirit for about three years.

The reason was that he had not set a time or place. Together we said it was to be tonight. "What we say is what we get," and "what we picture is what we believe." We said it, and then we pictured it. He had already received the filling of the Holy Spirit, and his remarkably changed life was a proof of it. Together we pictured the release of his spirit so that the Holy Spirit could come flooding over him, enveloping and baptising him in his power.

He asked the Lord Jesus to baptise him with his Holy Spirit and he pictured the Holy Spirit descending upon him as a great glowing light. He did not need to delay, as the Holy Spirit has been available since Pentecost. Now we accept by faith that the Spirit comes upon us. I asked my friend, "Do you believe He has done this now?" He said, "Yes." "Then do not delay any longer," I exhorted him. "Begin speaking in the new prayer language He has for you."

Why the prayer language? Because in this gift you have the greatest measure of control. In fact, you can will to speak it, or withhold it with your own free will.

How and why? Jesus Himself in his last words gave you the authority of his name to do so in *Mark 16:17* (New Trans.). Read it like this: "And those that believe (you are a believer?) shall use the authority of Jesus' name ... to speak in new languages." Moreover, this gift is the key to moving into all the other gifts. This is the gift that more than any other gives you the assurance that the Holy Spirit is baptising you – present continuous tense. This is the gift that charges you spiritually and helps to keep you charged. *1 Corinthians 14:4* says: "He who speaks in an unknown tongue edifies himself (or better, charges himself)" and if you keep on using the "prayer language" you keep on charging yourself in the same way that your alternator keeps charging your car battery.

So, my friend and I, having set the time and place, decided that the matter would not be put off to the eternal tomorrow, and we opened our mouths. I began to use my prayer language softly, but clearly, near him and he, with an open mouth, said nothing! I explained again that though I had had ten years' experience of using the prayer language, I still don't know in advance what words would come out of my mouth. I still have to open my mouth and utter the words by faith. It always remains a faith language, not a learned language. I demonstrated this slowly, one word at a time. With a chuckle I suggested, "Are you going to put it off until tomorrow again?"

His reply was a definite, No! So we started again. It is no good just opening the mouth without speaking the words in faith. One thing is certain, the Holy Spirit will never speak through you of his own accord. We have to use our will and the authority of Jesus' name to speak the words ourselves as Jesus told us in *Mark 16:17* (LB).

I used my prayer language again, as this helps. I could hear sound coming hesitantly from him. Now that he had started I suggested he continue to speak out the words the Holy Spirit gave him until a greater fluency came. After half an hour's practice there was no doubt in him that he had received a prayer language. As it was late we went to bed. I urged him to use it again as soon as he opened his eyes in the morning!

As we use the prayer language, we stay charged throughout the day.

Since I have used the prayer language as much as I can throughout the day, even while doing my ordinary work, I can honestly say that I can't remember when I last had a bad day. As I pray in this language, the devil is afraid to come near because the Holy Spirit is continually protecting me. The prayer language is the most effective way I know to eliminate hindrances and problems. You see, our thoughts and words paint a picture inside which no one else sees. This constant communion with the Holy Spirit enables Him to give you a picture of what He wants to do through you. See God's picture of yourself.

What you begin to picture is what you are going to be able to believe! Faith leads to action!

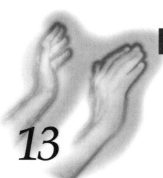

Do I have to speak in tongues in order to be baptised with the Holy Spirit?

13

Why should I ramble on with multiple explanations before coming to the point? Let us have the answer now! Well, the answer to the question posed is, "No"! My response was to a multi-racial, multi-denominational gathering.

Because of my emphatic "No", all the non-charismatics are pointing to the charismatics and Pentecostals and saying, "See, I told you so!" Some of the charismatics and Pentecostals are saying, not with venom, but with a little dismay, "Jack, how could you say 'No'?" Other charismatics are thoughtfully nodding their heads, but not saying anything.

Of course, this is all fantasy, if somewhat humorous. But there is some truth in it, isn't there?

What I don't like about the discussions are the divisions. After all, this is a united gathering of various denominations, including Catholics.

By the way, did you know that Pope John Paul's statistics showed at that time that there were 50 million charismatic catholic Christians throughout the world?

Jesus is our unity

Can't we start with unifying thoughts rather than divisive ones? After all, Jesus prayed for this unity in his great prayer for all his children in John Chapter 17.

Jesus is the sole unifying power in our relationships with one another. Speaking to His Father, Jesus said: "As you sent Me into the world, I have sent them (that's us) into the world. For them I sanctify Myself that they too may be truly sanctified." (Or, consecrated, set apart for God's service only.) *John 17:18–21.*

Such service is our obligation, whatever our theology. Jesus goes on in this selfless prayer for you and me: "That all of them (that's us again) may be one, Father, just as You are in Me and I am in You. May they also be in Us so that the world may believe that You have sent Me."

Are Christians one today? Alas, no. Let me ask a question. Can you think of any time in history when this prayer of Jesus was answered? It seems that it was true of the 120 at Pentecost. It seems it was true of the 3000 just after Pentecost, and for some period in the early church's history. But a little while later the Corinthian saints were saying, "I am of Apollos", others, "I am of Paul". What had happened? They were clinging to the divisive doctrines of men rather than to Jesus Himself. Why can't we all say, "I am of Jesus"? I think we can. We never argue about Jesus. He is our central theme. He is our Lord. He is our all.

We had a taste of this unity in the January of 1980, when 7 000 Christians of all colours and from many races in Africa gathered for a conference on the Holy Spirit in Johannesburg. Unity was very evident on that occasion. On the last evening, all denominations had communion together. Both Catholics and Protestants put aside their particular doctrines, and all had the Lord's Supper together. History was made in Africa that day. I had never experienced such unity. Two years before such a thing could not have happened, but things are now moving rapidly in answer to Jesus' prayer.

I believe that unity like this will happen increasingly before our Lord Jesus returns. This decade will see unprecedented unity. *John 17:21* tells us why: "So that the world may believe that You (Father) have sent Me." Jesus has made it possible because He has given us his glory. It makes no difference doctrinally, whether one says, "I am clothed by faith with God's glory," another, "I am baptised (or immersed) with God's Spirit," and another, "I am for the first time abiding in Christ".

He has clothed me with Himself." The Holy Spirit never claims glory for Himself, but only for Jesus. *John 16:14*: "He (the Holy Spirit) will bring glory to Me by taking what is mine and making it known to you."

Perhaps, in the past, you have thought: Will this prayer of Jesus be fulfilled only in heaven?" This, of course, is true, but in two scriptures Jesus said it would be answered on earth as well.

The one is quoted above, *John 17:21*, and the following Scripture is second: *John 17:23:* "May they (us again) be brought to complete unity, (why?) to let the world know that You sent Me, and have loved them, even as You have loved Me."

I am more sure now than ever that God the Father will answer this prayer of his dear Son, even if it is the last thing He does before Jesus comes back to the earth to take over the reins of world government. This will be the climax of the world revival already upon us.

Not only 7 000, but thousands upon thousands of Christians will throng stadiums to declare their unity with the Body of Christ. Thousands of Jews will be there, too. Catholics and Protestants will sink their differences and demonstrate oneness and love for Jesus. The adherents of other religions will say that Jesus is the one they had been looking for all along. Protestants are no longer protesting against anything.

What does this talk on unity have to do with the chapter heading? Simply this, that Jesus must first be our all; then nothing else will matter. If Jesus baptises us with his Holy Spirit and we submit to his baptism, that is all that matters. If Jesus gives us a heavenly language with which to praise Him, so much the better. Jesus is the Author of all that really matters. If we say that we are not baptised with the Holy Spirit until we have spoken in "tongues", we are making "tongues" part of the Baptism. "Tongues" is a gift of the Holy Spirit resulting from the baptism of God's Holy Spirit for power. Truly, "tongues" in biblical times was an evidence of the Holy Spirit's baptism, as it is now. Jesus said that power was another evidence of the Spirit's baptism. *Acts 1:8* (KJ) says: "Ye shall receive power after that the Holy Spirit has come upon you, and ye shall be witnesses unto Me."

Jesus is our great Unifier. He is our Oneness. We recognise and respect the differences of others. In our Messiah we never despise one another or any other denomination. All we are called to do is to love one another, not criticize one another.

We are one body in Christ

In the very chapter which speaks about the gifts of the Spirit and where the gift of "tongues" is included, the Bible speaks of the united Body of Christ. The Bible makes no mention of divisions, though it respects differences. "Tongues" is, of course, a prayer and praise language (1 Cor 14:2). What Christian has felt that he does not pray sufficiently, and praise our Heavenly Father adequately? You agree? Well, we should not criticise or argue against this gift of the Holy Spirit.

This is the one gift that enables us to pray and praise adequately. *1 Corinthians 12:12* says: "The body is a unit, though it is made up of many parts; and although its parts are many, they form one body. So is it with the Messiah, for we are all baptised by one Holy Spirit into one body, whether Jews or Greeks." May I add, "Whether Malawian or South African, Liberian or Japanese, Peruvian or American."

1 Corinthians 12:14–20 confirms: "Now the body is not made up of one part, but of many. If the foot should say, 'Because I am not a hand, I do not belong to the body', and if the ear should say, 'Because I am not an eye, I do not belong to the body,' ... If the whole body were an eye, where would the sense of hearing be? If the whole body were an ear, where would the sense of smell be? But, in fact, God has arranged the parts in the body, every one of them just as He wanted them to be. If they were all one part, where would the body be? As it is there are many parts, but one body."

What do we see here? The Holy Spirit has baptised us into one body, the body of Christ. Every Christian throughout the world is part of this one body, so there is no reason for divisions, or argument on spiritual things. At the same time it is stressed that each part is important and has a vital part to play in the Body of the Messiah. Do not in any way underestimate yourself. Begin to realise who you are.

If you don't play the part God intended for you, that part of the body will be defective. You are placed in the body just as He wanted you to be. You should be eager then, to find out what ministry you must fulfil. The flesh does not help here. How could we possibly do what is spiritual in the energy of the flesh? Being filled and baptised with the Holy Spirit will enable one to be led into a ministry. We are so important to Jesus; we cannot let Him down, can we?

1 Corinthians 6:20 (LB) says: "For God has bought you with a great price. So use every part of your body to give glory back to God, because He owns it." Such is the extent of our dedication to Him. What right have we to hold back any part of ourselves for our own use?

Is it desirable to speak in the prayer language?

Picture the scene in the lounge again. Do you see how relaxed the scene is? What might have become an evening of argument and condemnation has turned into one of concord. Why? Because Jesus stepped into the scene. Our "unifier" had arrived. The Head of our Body controlled the situation. Not one of us now condemns the other. *Romans 8:1* says: "There is now no condemnation for those who are in Christ Jesus." We are now saying, "Lord Jesus, if you want to use my tongue to pray a prayer through me, I am willing. I am a willing instrument for any gift which you want to manifest through me in a given situation to help another part of our body in need. You are my Head. I am going to be controlled by you."

Jesus said in *Mark 16:17*: "And these signs will accompany those who believe. In my Name they will drive out demons; they will speak in new tongues." Not one of us will deny that the name of Jesus has authority. We can, if we wish, go right ahead, using the authority of the name of Jesus, and speak in a new prayer language.

If you do not wish to, Jesus will not force you to. But He will say: "My child, if you want the baptism of the Holy Spirit upon you without the prayer language, you can have this anointing on you. My difficulty is that without the prayer language pouring through you I have got the limitations of your own mind to contend with.

"Your prayer life will be spasmodic and lacking in dedication. You will admit that your mind has limitations, while I have infinite knowledge. Your limitations will make it very difficult for Me to increase the level of the filling of My Holy Spirit within you, let alone the anointing of the baptism of My Holy Spirit upon you. In fact, your experience of My Spirit working within you in power will be very restricted. I want to make it easier for you My child, I can bypass your mind, and you can pray effortlessly from your spirit. Will you not trust Me in this area of your life? You have been a believer in many areas of your life, now believe Me in this area too. You know My Name has power and authority. Now use this authority, and utter the strange words. My Spirit who lives in you will enable you to speak words which you will not understand, but they will come from the Spirit Who makes no mistakes with the words you utter. Do not be disappointed with your first efforts. Improvement will come with practice, like everything else worthwhile.

"Practise in private, and I will be with you to reassure you and to build you up in your faith and enlarge your vocabulary.

"I need an army of prayer warriors who will thus dedicate themselves to this ministry as there is so much to be done before My near return. Many of My children are hindered from receiving this gift of the prayer language, because they hold on to a deep-seated spirit of unforgiveness, resentment and rebellion.

"These sins in My eyes are like the sin of witchcraft." *1 Samuel 15:23*: "If you truly desire to become a channel for My Spirit, I can uncover these areas of foothold to the enemy. Ask Me and I will do it.

"I am calling My children to enter this ministry of prayer in the Spirit and to lead a life of repentance. Do not fear, for My blood has power to cleanse you, and deliver you from all unrighteousness.

"My child, hear My call, for great will be your reward.

"Together we will war against the prince of all wickedness, and My Spirit will be poured out to gather in the great harvest and unite My family into an unparalleled oneness before My return. My Father has promised Me this glory, but I need you whom I bought at a great price, and I need you now!

"My words have been plain. There is no mistaking my plea. Indeed, I have commanded My children to repent and to live a life baptised with My Spirit. Disobey Me, and I will not punish you in this the day of My grace, but you will reap what you sow.

"Obey Me with a willing heart and the baptism of My Spirit will be upon you with power."

To those not familiar with the type of message that has just been written, this is prophecy. The words of Jesus were not premeditated. Every word must be uttered by faith.

Prophecy like this is not infallible, but Scripture is. *1 Corinthians 13:9* (KJ) reads: "For we know in part, and we prophesy in part."

Prophecy is defined in *1 Corinthians 14:3:* (KJ): "But he that prophesieth speaketh unto men to edification, and exhortation, and comfort," or, in modern language, "But he who prophesies speaks to men for their strengthening, encouragement and comfort."

Prophecy should not then condemn. It will never go against scripture, but it must be tested against God's Word. Its message will consistently strengthen, give encouragement and comfort.

Being spoken in the first person will give it immediate authenticity. To say that prophecy and tongues have ceased is not supported by Scripture. God's Word says in *1 Corinthians 13:8*: "But where there are prophecies, they will cease; where there are tongues they will be stilled." When will they cease? (v. 10) "When perfection comes, when He that is perfect is come." The only One who has been perfect in all history is our Jesus. When He returns, communication will be perfect, just as his was with the Father, for we shall be like Him. Hallelujah!

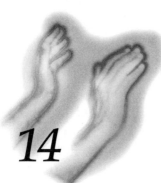

The prayer language for intercession

14

Eight of the past giants in prayer

I have read of great men of prayer whose lives have greatly impressed me. Let me quote what some of them made a habit of doing for most of their lives:

Martin Luther said: "If I fail to spend two hours in prayer each morning, the devil gets the victory through the day. When I have extra business, I cannot get on without spending three hours daily in prayer."

John Wesley began his day at four in the morning and spent at least two hours in prayer.

John Knox always rose early to pray, but often rose at odd hours in the night to pray in the little side room he used for prayer. I personally have spent a little time in that side room which juts out beyond the outside wall and from where he could look out over Edinburgh.

Archbishop Leighton was so much alone with God that he seemed to be in perpetual meditation. "Prayer and praise were his business and pleasure," says his biographer.

Edward Payson wore the hardwood boards into grooves where his knees pressed so often and so long.

Bishop Andrewes spent the greater part of five hours every day in prayer and devotion.

Yes, these were great men of prayer, but none impresses me more than David Brainerd and John Hyde, better known as "Praying Hyde".

David Brainerd was a missionary to the Indians in America. It is said of him that his whole life was a life of prayer. He prayed by day and by night. Before preaching and after preaching he prayed. Riding through the solitude of the forest he prayed. In the snow he prayed with such fervour that his brow was wet with sweat. God used him for a revival amongst the American people.

"Praying Hyde" was a missionary to the Punjab region in India, and was in fact one of the founders of the Punjab Prayer Union in 1904. Some of the points he made were, "Are you longing for greater power of the Holy Spirit in your own life and work? Are you convinced that you cannot go on without his power? Will you set apart at least one half-hour each day to pray until revival comes?" I like the way he at times involved others in a prolonged time of prayer.

R. McCheyne Paterson and "Praying Hyde" prayed for a revival in the church in India for thirty days and nights before the first Sialkot Convention. George Turner joined them for 21 of these days of prayer. 'Praying Hyde' said: "Self must be crucified, and be buried with Christ. If the 'old nature' is not buried, the stench of it will frighten souls away."

He was led to trust God first for one soul per day, then two, and lastly four souls per day. That was in 1910, and God took him all over India, preaching in the larger centres. He would often spend half the night in prayer. His prayers did not take in only India, but in a vision he says he saw "God's great battle for India and beyond, in China, Japan and Africa." No doubt his prayers are still being answered today.

When he left for India by ship, his uncle wrote a letter to him, saying, "I shall not cease praying for you, dear John, until you are filled with the Holy Spirit." This annoyed John. To think that he was not filled! Yet he knew that victory was not complete in his own life. He felt miserable for three days. Then the crisis came when he laid his life before the Lord and asked God to fill him with his Holy Spirit. In one of his sermons he said: "God is saying, 'Who will go for us, whom shall I send? Who will be his intercessors?'" If we are willing to put ourselves into God's hands, then God is willing to use us. But there are two conditions before He can do this – obedience and purity. This is saying no to your own will, and yes to God's. You are purified by the fire of the Holy Spirit."

"Praying Hyde" loved *Isaiah 61*, for he said he loved to receive God's oil for his mourning, his garment of praise for his own spirit of heaviness. He believed in praising and thanking God in everything.

At the Sialkot Convention, when more than two thousand people were present, "Praying Hyde" was one of the speakers. His messages were delivered with tremendous power. He did not fast for the merit it would bring, and he sometimes spent three days and nights in the prayer room without going to bed. In between praying he would be leading souls to the Lord.

He would be so full of joy that first one would see his body begin to move, then his feet and soon he would be dancing for joy. Others would join him, until the whole place would be ringing with praises to God! Am I speaking about a way-out Pentecostal?

No, a conservative Presbyterian, as he was.

These glimpses of John Hyde's life are from a book on his life edited by Captain E.G. Garre. What an inspiration to prayer! A life indeed dedicated to God.

What about us?

A life like that seems impossible for me. If I pray for ten minutes in English, that is about as much as I can manage. What do you say about yourself? Is it possible to measure up to these giants in prayer? We admire them, they inspire us to do more.

My trouble is to know what more I can pray about after I have prayed for ten minutes. Even if I set myself to pray for the countries of the world while looking at a map of the world, I know that I can pray little longer than ten minutes. But at best these would be general prayers. They no doubt would do so some good. What I pray about one country may have nothing to do with God's longing and infinite wisdom for that country. How may we, as average Christians, improve our prayer life, and even approach the depth of a "Praying Hyde"?

I believe God has provided the answer. I believe that it is wrapped up in a little package that Jesus did not unwrap for us in *John 4:23–24*. These verses have been quoted before, but let us look at them again: "Yet a time is coming and has now come when the true worshippers will worship the Father in spirit and in truth, for they are the kind of worshippers the Father seeks. God is Spirit, and His worshippers must worship Him in spirit and in truth (reality)."

So we believe our Messiah when He says that the Father seeks those who will worship Him in two ways, "in spirit and in truth". Jesus implied that up to that time no one had worshipped God in spirit, but that the time was coming and had already come for that. The question then is, how do we worship God in spirit and in truth?

The answer is to be found in *1 Corinthians 14:14–15*: "For if I pray in a tongue, my spirit prays, but my mind is unfruitful. So what shall I do? (I will pray both ways) I will pray with my spirit (that is, by the Holy Spirit within me) but I will also pray with my mind." This is what is meant by praying "in spirit and in truth". No wonder God says in *1 Corinthians 14:5*: "I would like everyone of you to pray in tongues", and why Paul says in *1 Corinthians 14:18*, "I thank my God I pray in tongues (privately) more than all of you."

Did Paul then have a secret that all these other great prayer warriors missed out on? I think he did. It was a secret that enabled him to pray more than anyone else without appearing to spend long hours in prayer. It enabled him to do other things while praying. He made tents with his hands while he prayed in the spirit, the Holy Spirit within him giving him the words. At the same time his mind was preparing the message he was going to preach that night. Three things at once!

This is *the* great secret God has for a multitude of the prayer warriors that He wants to recruit in these last days. I pray that everyone who reads this book may make a quality decision to become a prayer warrior of this kind. No one else will know that you spend long hours in prayer. While you are preparing the breakfast or cooking the evening meal, you will be praying in the spirit. While you are driving the car, mowing the lawn, working for your firm, reading a book, or, as Oral Roberts does, while shaving! The opportunities are endless. You will make the effort to pray in the prayer language whatever else you are doing, even when writing. I have even been told by someone that he was woken up praying in the prayer language!

God is going to raise up an army of prayer warriors who will pray in the spirit, with the Holy Spirit directing the whole operation. This is what will bring about the greatest ingathering of souls that the world has ever seen, a oneness of believers and a world revival. So, get rid of your bias against "tongues" right now or you might be left out of God's great army of prayer warriors! Stop worrying about the finesse of your prayer language. We are not responsible for the sounds that come out of our mouths. All we have to do is make the sounds.

The Holy Spirit is responsible for the form it takes, as He gives the utterance. Be content to leave that responsibility to Him. Surely we can have faith in the Spirit of God! As God has promised, it will be bread and not a stone. It will be a prayer language from Him and nothing else. God says of this gift that we speak directly to Him: "For anyone who speaks in a tongue does not speak to men but to God ... He utters mysteries (secret words) with his spirit" *(1 Cor 14:2)*. He would like everyone to use his gift. He says in 1 Corinthians 14:5: "I (God) would like everyone of you to speak in tongues."

Jesus says that if we qualify as a believer, we can go ahead and speak out in this language, using the authority of his name *(Mark 16:17)*. People like to "be with it". This is the modern way of intercession directed by the Holy Spirit. He knows what we should pray for. We don't, because our minds are not infinite.

At the close of this chapter a list of 50 advantages of using the prayer language will be given.

Let me give just one illustration which opened up the whole of God's plan for the use of his secret weapon, the prayer language for me.

God's secret weapon

Dr. John Kuhne was a lecturer in veterinary science at Onderstepoort, north of Pretoria, at the time of this particular experience. He became pastor of the Bedfordview Baptist Church in Johannesburg. Later he went to Hawaii with "Youth with a Mission".

While John was a deacon in the Hatfield Baptist Church, he prayed quietly for our pastor Ed, as he started preaching. Suddenly his prayer became so earnest that it could only be described as deep travail, such was the feeling being transmitted by the Holy Spirit to his body. John yielded to the prayer with inward groans. His first thoughts were that he was praying for the Word of God to have free course and power through Ed's preaching. The prayer was of such unusual depth that he was prompted to ask the Lord, "But Lord, what am I praying for?"

The Lord answered him in a vision before his closed eyes. He saw an angry sea and his eyes became focused on an upturned boat. All around were people trying to grip onto the slippery sides of the boat without much hope of succeeding. Others were already drowning. Over on the right were two men who were beginning to swim away.

He noticed that they had brown bodies and longish black hair. He wondered what nationality they were, and the thought came to him, "I wonder if they are perhaps Indonesians." As the vision passed before him, God said to him in his thoughts, "You are praying for these two men. Pray on earnestly for them for I want them to reach shore. I have a great work for them and I want them to be saved."

As the Lord mentioned the word "shore", John looked ahead in his vision and could see the outline of an island. At this point the vision began to fade and John prayed on earnestly, as if in travail, until the burden began to lift. A joy swept over him and he felt that through prayer in the spirit he had received the answer to what God had urged him to pray for.

Driving home in the car after the service, John related his experience to his wife and family. The next day, on Monday afternoon, his wife was scanning the *Pretoria News* when she saw a small news item. It read: "Jakarta. Twenty-one wedding guests drowned in angry sea when a boat capsized in the Java Straits. Two men managed to swim ashore to Pailang Island." It was a Sapa-Reuter news item.

She thought, "This is what John prayed about so earnestly. The two men did reach the shore. How wonderful! It even mentions the name of the island."

When John arrived home she said, "John, come and look at this." He read the news item and said: "But this is exactly what I saw in the vision, and here it says that the two men reached Pailang Island. Well, praise the Lord! Here in the newspaper is the answer to the prayer which the Holy Spirit was urging me to pray. I saw the actual event as it was happening on Sunday!"

As John told the story, one thing puzzled me. Why did God use John, sitting 7 000 km away, and not one of the revived Christians in Indonesia? We had heard of the wonderful revival God had poured out on those parts. I decided to go to the Lord and ask Him a direct question. I said, "Lord, would you explain to me why you used John Kuhne so far away when surely you could have used one of the thousands of revived Christians in Indonesia? This seems more logical to me."

I was using the prayer language, and the Lord gave me this equally direct reply. I repeated his words from what came to me in a thought pattern: "The eyes of the Lord run to and fro throughout the whole earth to show Myself strong on behalf of those whose hearts are perfect towards me.

"My eyes ran through Indonesia and I found no one. My eyes continued to run through the world and I found John sitting in the Hatfield Baptist Church in Pretoria, South Africa. He was already through to Me, praying in the spirit. He was ready for the instant prayer burden I needed to save those two men. I diverted his prayer language for this particular need. The Holy Spirit prayed for all the necessary details to save those two men."

Clearly it is desirable to use the prayer language. Do you agree?

The reason for intercession

This aspect opened up a whole new world of prayer to me. I could see now why God requires our bodies to be the temple of the Holy Spirit. God wants to do so much for us but He can't legally do it on earth unless the request comes from one of his children who live on the earth. The devil took the earth from Adam by deception. Adam gave all his rights of dominion over the earth to the devil. He disobeyed God, the King of righteousness, and obeyed the Evil One, the king of all disobedience and rebellion against God.

Do you remember the temptation of Jesus in *Matthew 4:8*: "The devil took Jesus to a very high mountain and showed Him all the kingdoms of the world and their splendour. 'All this will I give you,' he said, 'if you bow down and worship me.'"

Jesus did not dispute the devil's lease upon the world, but let us never forget that Jesus defeated the devil and bought back all we had lost when Adam sinned. *Colossians 2:15* says: "And having disarmed the powers and authorities, he made a public spectacle of them, triumphing over them by the cross." We now have to hold the devil to his defeat and take back these kingdoms by the authority of Jesus' name.

Where is the fight to take place to win back what has rightly been purchased by Jesus? Jesus said in *Matthew 28:18–19*: "All authority in heaven and earth has been given to me, therefore go and make disciples of all nations." We have so little knowledge of all nations and all the kingdoms of the earth. Let us admit this and place ourselves at God's disposal to be used in the miracle prayer language. In "tongues" we pray the words the Holy Spirit gives. He has all the knowledge we lack. Our call is to fervent prayer before Jesus comes.

Christians must not apathetically give countries and kingdoms over to the devil. We are the ones who have authority over the devil and his deception in the name of Jesus. *2 Chronicles 7:14* reads: "If My people who are called by My Name will humble themselves and pray and seek My face and turn from their wicked ways, then I will hear from heaven and will forgive their sin and will heal their land" – purchased by the blood of Jesus. I added the last part to lend force to what Jesus has really done for us.

We Christians must get forceful, but against whom? The devil, of course! We must not let the devil take over our own country, or any other country such as Zimbabwe, Zambia, Angola, Mozambique, Liberia, or even China. We must stand with the Christians in all the countries of the world and put fresh courage into them and a new fighting spirit.

You say, how can I pray for people who live half way round the world? I don't have the knowledge. I'm just a weak Christian. Stop saying things like this to your inward man, your spirit. Jesus said in *Matthew 11:11*: "The least in the kingdom of heaven is greater than John the Baptist. Now how could we be greater than John the Baptist, that fiery, fearless preacher? Jesus said again in *Matthew 11:11*: "Among those born of women there has not risen anyone greater than John the Baptist. "Do you mean he was greater than Moses or Elijah?

Well, we must believe Jesus. We must also believe Jesus when He says, "Dear blood-bought child of God, even though you think yourself to be the least, you are greater than John the Baptist." Start believing what Jesus has said of you. Jesus believes in you. No, we will not boast, but neither will we entertain negative thoughts about ourselves, nor will we be building on sand.

In *Matthew 7:26* Jesus says, "But everyone who hears these word of mine, and does not put them into practice is like a foolish man who built his house on sand." After reading these powerful words, which one of us feels like disobeying Jesus, and building on sand?

If we keep on thinking negatively and talking negatively to our inward man, the spiritual man will never grow. This is the great value of the prayer language. You can tell when Christians start using the prayer language. How? Because they begin to grow fast.

You ask me why? I think God is telling me why. Because the Holy Spirit never accuses you, never disparages you. He builds you up. He speaks to your inward man and tells you what Jesus thinks of you. Jesus knows what He can make of you, and He wants you to come up to that level. Most of us pay more attention to all the negative rubbish the devil feeds into us. It is unmerciful, the way he can accuse us. This is one thing I know, friends. When I am using the prayer language, I can never hear the devil.

If this chapter does one thing, I hope it is this: I have faith that it will gain another recruit to use the prayer language in these last days before Jesus comes!

Fifty advantages of using the prayer language

Mark 16:17 says: "All believers may use the authority of Jesus' Name to speak in this unlearned language by faith." *1 Corinthians 14:1* says: "Eagerly desire it."

1. You are able with a little practice to pray in tongues while reading the Bible. Try it! (Rom 8:26(b))
1a. This prayer from the Holy Spirit is not limited to the mind.
2. The Holy Spirit is the author. (Rom 8:26(a))
3. It refreshes physically and spiritually. (Isa 40:31; Neh 8:10)
4. It is prayer completely in the Lord's will. (Rom 8:27)
5. It will be answered positively. (Rom 8:27)
6. It is our private "hot line" to the Father. (1 Cor 14:2)
7. If we ask, we can have a private answer back from God. (1 Cor 14:13)
8. Prayer language and answer restores easy communion with God. (1 Cor 14:2, 13)
9. Ask and God can give you a mind picture of your prayer.

10. You can pray while doing other work. (1 Cor 14:15)
11. Prayer not from the mind opens the way to praying without ceasing. (1 Thes 5:17)
12. You can pray for hours without tiring. (Isa 28:11–12)
13. Mind wandering is no problem – pray audibly, in a whisper.
14. This way deep travailing prayer is not exhausting. (Gal 14:19)
15. It drives out fear. (2 Tim 1:7)
16. Devastating to pride, that is, not from self, but from the Holy Spirit.
17. Roots of bitterness can't take hold. (1 Cor 14:4)
18. Feeds faith to your heart. (Rom 14:23; Jude 20)
19. It tames the wicked tongue. (Jas 3:5–10)
20. The easiest, and finest way of intercessory prayer. (Rom 8:26)
21. The way to bring world revival. (2 Chron 7:14)
22. You become part of the Holy Spirit's plan. (1 Cor 14:14)
23. It is praying by faith and therefore pleasing to God. (Heb 11:6)
24. Exalts God rather than self. (1 Cor 14:2)
25. Expresses what you feel in your heart towards God. (1 Cor 14:14–16)
26. You can bless God more adequately with your spirit. (1 Cor 14:16)
27. Thanks and praise to God at last can be adequate. (1 Cor 14:17)
28. It is not restricted in private use – many hours are possible. (1 Cor 14:18)
29. It is a complete and closely guarded secret. (1 Cor 14:2)
30. Neither the devil nor other people can understand it. (1 Cor 14:2)
31. The devil can't hinder this prayer. (See Dan 10:12–21.)
32. We who are ignorant can pray with God's wisdom. (1 Cor 14:14)
33. The Father wants worship in spirit and in truth. (John 4:23–24)
34. God needs those who will dedicate themselves to this vital prayer. (John 4:23–24)
35. It helps quick spiritual growth. (1 Cor 14:4)
36. It develops your spiritual intellect. (1 Cor 14:8)
37. Opens you up to God's knowledge. (1 Cor 14:4, 13)
38. The things of God are made more clear. (1 Cor 14:4, 13)
39. The key used by the Holy Spirit to lead one into all the gifts.
40. Keeps you filled and baptised with the Holy Spirit. (Eph 5:19)
41. Gives a deep inner therapy, and release of spirit, soul and body. (John 4:24)

42. Not a sign of superiority, but of your own inadequacy and reliance on the Holy Spirit.

43. Criticism so easy in our language is impossible in the prayer language.

44. It is a language of the born-again spirit. Don't stifle it.

45. It is the attacking weapon of God's armour. Praying in spirit. (Eph 6:18)

46. We do obey God "I would like everyone of you to pray in tongues." (1 Cor 14:5)

47. The emphasis is on private prayer. Restrictions are only in church. (1 Cor 14:18, 27)

48. It is imperative – a "must" – said our Jesus. (John 4:24)

49. It is an evidence of the baptism of the Holy Spirit. (Acts 10:44, 46)

50. Keeps you "charged" – (edified) with the Holy Spirit. But only as you use the prayer language.

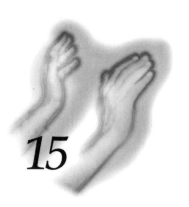

Reaching out for the gifts

15

Misapprehensions about the gifts

Just as the fruit of the Holy Spirit is associated with the filling of the Holy Spirit, so the gifts of the Holy Spirit are associated with the baptism of the Holy Spirit. It was so in the life of Jesus, and it is true in the lives of his children as well. This was explained at length in the previous chapters.

Even if you know that you are filled with the Holy Spirit, remember that even Jesus was not used in the gifts before He was baptised with the Holy Spirit. Your experience should surely not be greater than his. Be immersed with the Holy Spirit by faith first, then the gifts will follow. If you try to put the gifts first, you will fall into the trap of confusing natural gifts with the supernatural gifts of the Holy Spirit.

Who is Jesus' representative on earth now? Of course your answer is: the Holy Spirit. Then we should give the Holy Spirit his rightful first place in our lives. When people speak of the gifts of the Holy Spirit, they usually turn to the epistle to the Corinthians. I should like at the outset to point out an interesting aspect in this epistle which often forms a barrier for Christians desiring the gifts of the Holy Spirit. It is often said, "If this is what the gifts did for the Corinthians, then I don't need them. I prefer the fruit of the Holy Spirit." But it is not a matter of one or the other. To be truly effective in God's work we need both, just as a pair of scissors needs two blades.

A dove is said to have nine main feathers on each wing. The nine on one wing correspond to the nine fruits of the Spirit. The nine on the other wing are likened to the nine special gifts of the Holy Spirit. For a balanced Christian life we need both wings.

The interesting point I want to make is this. The Corinthians had the gifts of the Holy Spirit, but they neglected the fruit. They had the baptism with the Holy Spirit but lacked the filling. Many of our present-day Pentecostal churches have realised this and are now stressing the necessity of having our lives cleansed by the blood of Jesus, so that we might be filled with the Holy Spirit, and thus bear the fruit of the Spirit.

Paul, in writing to the Corinthian believers, at first commends them as in *1 Corinthians 1:5, 7*: "In Jesus you have been enriched in every way. Therefore you do not lack any spiritual gift." Note: They did not lack gifts, but they lacked the fruit.

Then Paul reveals the real purpose of his letter, which is not to praise them: "Dear brothers, I have been talking to you as though you were still just babies in the Christian life, who are not following the Lord, but your own desires; I cannot speak to you as I would to healthy Christians who are filled with the Holy Spirit" (*1 Cor 3:1*). This verse sums up the drift of the whole epistle. These Christians needed to be filled with God's Spirit.

Even when it came to the gifts of the Holy Spirit, Paul needed to remind them that they had to use them for helping others, not for their own selfish ends. The use of the prayer language was to be strictly limited to three persons in any one church meeting (*1 Cor 14:27*). Then each had to be interpreted. In the operation of all the gifts, "Everything should be done in a fitting and orderly way" (*1 Cor 14:40*). We dare not disobey God's instructions.

The gifts are to be regarded as the power tools of the Church

The fact that they are not being used correctly by one church is no reason for disallowing their use elsewhere. We have God's strict instructions for their use in *1 Corinthians 14:39*: "My brothers, be eager to prophesy, and do not forbid speaking in tongues." We must remember that these are the gifts of the Holy Spirit that we are speaking about. If we spurn his gifts, we can't think much of the Giver. This is terribly dangerous ground, because we can unknowingly be grieving the Holy Spirit. None of us wants to do that, do we?

Many Christians have been prevented from reaching out for the gifts because *1 Corinthians 12:31* seems to indicate that there is a more excellent way which supersedes the gifts, and that is love.

What this verse really says is that all the gifts of the Holy Spirit must be used with love, and never harshly. The New International Version puts the first part of this Scripture very strongly: "But eagerly desire the greater gifts." This is God's will. We must not be robbed of the gifts. God wants us to desire them eagerly.

The next half of the verse says, "And now I will show you the most excellent way." This does not contradict the first half, but it means to convey that the gifts must be operated with love.

The Living Bible, which I love, has conveyed a misconception here. *1 Corinthians 12:31* (LB) reads: "No, but try your best to have the more important of these gifts. First, however, let me tell you about something else that is better than any of them." This refers to the gifts. A contradiction is introduced with those last words. It implies that love is better than any of the gifts. I hope the publishers will change it. An acceptable rendering would be: "Eagerly desire the more important of these gifts. First, however, let me tell you of something that is essential for exercising all of them! That is Love."

In *1 Corinthians 14:1* we are urged by God's Word to "Follow the way of love and eagerly desire spiritual gifts, especially the gift of prophecy."

It seems unnecessary to mention the old favourite argument held by some that the gifts have ceased anyway. This is, of course, false doctrine. No scripture supports this argument. What *1 Corinthians 13:8* does say is that "Love never fails. But where there are prophecies, they will cease; where there are tongues, they will be stilled; where there is knowledge, it will pass away."

Let us note that it says 'will pass away' and not has already done so. The inference is that gifts will be done away with when perfection comes (v. 10). Who is perfect? I know of only one perfect one, don't you? Our Messiah.

Which gifts should I reach out for?

The old idea was that the Holy Spirit gave one gift to Jack, another to Mary, and, if Peter was especially gifted, he was probably given two. James at the bottom of the ladder probably had to be satisfied with none, since the Holy Spirit "divides to every man severally as He will" (1 Cor 12:11).

But this is not the way the Holy Spirit distributes his gifts. The New International Version says: "All these gifts are the work of one and the same Spirit, and He gives them to each man, just as He determines." He does not leave anyone out. "He gives to each person".

That is why we are told on two occasions to "eagerly desire spiritual gifts." If we desire them for ourselves, we shall certainly not receive. On the other hand, if we desire them to help someone in need, our motive will be right, and we shall receive accordingly. The Holy Spirit knows our motives and for this reason He determines which gift is needful for a particular occasion. Nobody takes that sovereign privilege from the Holy Spirit. It is his prerogative.

If you are willing to be used by the Holy Spirit, all these gifts are open to you, if you "eagerly desire them".

An interesting point is that when you are experiencing the gifts, the Holy Spirit seems to combine many of the gifts. Often one can't tell where the one begins and another ends.

The other most interesting concept is that the Holy Spirit gives nine gifts. Jesus also has gifts that He gives to his Church. They appear to number thirteen but could also be fourteen. The Father in His love is very generous with His gifts, they number eighteen.

Let us have a look at these gifts.

The gifts (charismata) of the Holy Spirit and the gifts of Jesus

The nine gifts are manifestations of the Holy Spirit, *1 Corinthians 12:3*: "No one speaking by the Spirit of God says, 'Jesus be cursed.' This Scripture is God's guarantee that nothing will be said out of place in "tongues".

We can divide the gifts into three categories:

1. Spoken gifts to enable us to speak more of what God says
2. Revelation gifts to enable us to know more of what God knows
3. Power gifts to enable us to do more of what God does.

The gifts of the Spirit – used in ministry to others (1 Cor 12:8–10)

Spoken gifts

1. Prayer languages	The "hot line" to God. Not understood by Satan. Under full control of the speaker. This gift is "tongues". Prayer and praise to God.
2. Interpretation	(Replication). God's reply to the "prayer language".
3. Prophecy	Also *Romans 12:6*. Never condemnatory, but God's channel to strengthen, encourage, and comfort. Only foretells something when combined with the word of wisdom.

Revelation gifts

4. Word of wisdom	Words of God-given advice, and against which there is no argument. Revealed wisdom tells of the future.

5. Word of knowledge	A fragment of God's knowledge, which can come in a vision, impression, words, feeling, such as pain or inward perception. Knowledge of the past up to the present.
6. Discerning of spirits	Whether evil spirits are attacking the person from within or from without. By contrast to discern when the Holy Spirit is at work.

Power gifts

7. Gift of faith	Usually follows word of knowledge. A knowing inside. Must be acted on.
8. Gifts of healing	Follows the gift of faith. Both gifts operate best when the gift of faith is both in the receiver and the one who prays.
9. Gifts of miracles	

The gifts of Jesus to his church. Gifts we can become.

The five-fold ministry

1. Apostles	1 Corinthians 12:28; Ephesians 4:11. Special messengers, *ministry* Missionaries marked by signs, wonders, miracles. 2 Corinthians 12:12
2. Prophets	1 Corinthians 12:28, 14:3; Ephesians 4:11. Speak to strengthen, encourage and comfort.
3. Teachers	1 Corinthians 12:28; Romans 12:7; Ephesians 4:11. Those with a gift to teach without error.
4. Evangelists	Ephesians 4:11. A preacher for winning souls, or a gifted personal soul winner.
5. Pastors	Ephesians 4:11. Shepherds of the flock, who also teach, evangelise and preach.

1 Corinthians 12:28. The following five ministry gifts seem to be part of the above five as some are duplicated in *Ephesians 4:11*. Added evidence is that *1 Corinthians 12:5* says: "There are different kinds of service ministries but the same Lord. " The name 'Lord' refers to Jesus.

6. Workers of miracles	*1 Corinthians 12:28*. These two gifts apply to gifted.
7. Gifts of healing	Persons given to the church. It seems to apply more often to the evangelist. *Acts 8:4–8.*

8. Helpers	"Ministry of "helps". 1 Corinthians 12:28. An assistant. No limit. Counsellors, prayer warriors, helpers in all kinds of work, compassionate, unselfish. The gift with which to start!
9. Administrative ability	1 Corinthians 12:28. God-given, never domineering. Governments. A quality of leadership. One who guides or leads. A director. An organiser. One whose wise counsel you can rely on. One in government who can guide a Nation under God.
10. Different kinds of tongues	1 Corinthians 12:28. Here "tongues" is different from one's "Prayer Language" used in private. It applies to ministry in a gathering of believers, and should be followed by interpretation. 1 Corinthians 14:26–27

Four more gifts seem to belong under this heading, as they apply to ministry in Christ's Church and are very common in charismatic churches.

11. Singing in tongues	1 Corinthians 14:15. Holy Spirit inspired singing in multiple praise to God. This often forms part of worship.
12. Visions	Acts 9:3–5, Paul. Acts 10:3–6, Cornelius. Acts 10:11–16, Peter. Acts 2:17 A promise, especially to young people. Usually on the screen of one's mind. See also Lamentations 2:9. Proverbs 29:18
13. Revelation	1 Corinthians 14:26. God-given information beyond human wisdom. A sudden understanding of God's Word.
14. Music and song	Musicians and those gifted in song. Psalmists like David in the Old Testament.

Nineteen gifts from the Father. Motive gifts to equip you in Christ's body

1. Prophesying	Romans 12:6. Preaching under the Holy Spirit's anointing. Preaching. The good communicator.
2. Serving	Romans 12:7, 1 Peter 4:11. (1) Meeting the practical needs of others. (2) Helping others in their spiritual needs.
3. Teaching	Romans 12:7. To enjoy studying the Word and teaching others.

4. Encouraging	Romans 12:8, Hebrews 3:13. "Encourage one another daily."
5. Generous giving	Romans 12:8, 2 Corinthians 9:11. "You will be made rich in every way so that you can be generous on every occasion."
6. Leadership	Romans 12:8. A good Leader finds out God's plan first, then inspires others to reach the same goal.
7. Mercy	Romans 12:8. Tender-hearted and full of compassion like Jesus. Comforting others.
8. Love 'Agape'	Romans 12:9, 10, 1 Peter 4:8. God's love imparted to you through the Holy Spirit. Romans 5:5. It never fails. 1 Corinthians 13:8
9. Spiritual fervour	Romans 12:11. Bubbling with earnest zeal and Holy Spiritual energy.
10. Hope	Romans 12:12. Hope gives you the long range vision to bring you into faith.
11. Patience in trouble Perseverance	Romans 12:12. Patience and perseverance keep you in faith until you receive what you prayed for. Hebrews 10:35, 36
12. The intercessor Faithful in prayer	Romans 12:12, 1 Corinthians 14:5 (New Trans.). "I desire everyone of you to pray in tongues." See Romans 8:26, 27
13. Hospitality	Romans 12:13, 1 Peter 4:8. Opening your home and sharing what you have with others.
14. Blessing	Romans 12:14. To radiate joy and blessing others. The opposite to cursing.
15. Empathy	Romans 12:1 5. The ability to enter into the emotions of others, and sharing with them.
16. Live in harmony	Romans 12:16. This person brings a little bit of heaven to earth.
17. Humility	Romans 12:16. This person is not class and colour conscious but treats all with equal kindness. Bold, but not proud.
18. Do not take revenge	Romans 12:17–21. Living at peace with everyone. "Leave room for God's wrath."
19. Speaking gracious words from God	1 Peter 4:11. This is different from preaching. Colossians 3:16: One in whom "the Word of Christ dwells richly."

The nineteen motivational gifts

These gifts will be most evident in the end time revival. Why do I say this? They are now coming into prominence, and are part of the "restoration of all things" (*Acts 3:21*). They are the gifts the Father gives which enable you to identify your place in the body of Christ, so that you know what to do in life. For you to function to the best of your ability you must know what your main calling in life is. If you don't know, you often feel frustrated, and you lack a goal and motivation in your Christian life. Once other Christians understand what your calling is, you can be respected in that area instead of being misunderstood.

Study this carefully, looking up the scriptures where you suspect your gift may be. Ask the Holy Spirit to lead you, and concentrate on developing your gift. All nineteen gifts apply to you, but you will excel in a few.

1. Prophesying-preaching-communicating (Rom 12:6)

Thayer's Greek Lexicon tells us that this is preaching by Divine inspiration and declares the purposes of God. It is also reproving, comforting, and revealing hidden truths (*2 Tim 4:2; Gal 2:7*). Liddell and Scott say it is the exposition of scripture, public instruction or preaching the message of God. It is inspired preaching. Strong says it is, "to proclaim the Word." *1 Corinthians 12:10* contains the identical word *"Prophetia"*. Is it the same? *1 Corinthians 14:3* tells us that it is a message to strengthen, encourage and comfort. I asked the Lord about it, and He said the difference was that *1 Corinthians 12:10* was a special manifestation of the Holy Spirit, whereas *Romans 12:6* was the motivational gift planted in you by God. There could be a latent gift of preaching in you. Do not easily write yourself off in this area. Such a gift takes years to develop.

2. Serving others (1 Pet 4:11; Rom 12:7)

This is a gift of deeds. It delights in meeting the practical needs of others. Thayer's says of the word Diakonia, that it can be applied to preparing food, taking care of the poor or sick.

Are you a cook or a nurse, and enjoy it? Do you love fixing things? When asked to do something will you go the extra mile? This is the practical side, but according to Thayer's there is a spiritual side too.

Do you love to point someone to Jesus, to counsel someone and encourage them in their problems, and to lead them through to the baptism with the Holy Spirit? The office of a deacon is in this sphere.

3. Teaching (Rom 12:7)

This embodies a desire to study the Word, to find out the true meaning of words and to explain the result, even if it is to one person. It is to meditate on and receive revelation from the Word (*Gal 1:11, 12*). This person loves to pass God's Word on by teaching or writing (*2 Thes 2:15*). The one gifted in teaching should always rely on the instruction of the Holy Spirit in all things (*1 John 2:27* and *John 14:26*). Jesus is our best example. He taught with illustration, accuracy and authority. *Matthew 7:28, 29:* "When Jesus had finished saying these things the crowds were amazed at His teaching, because he taught as one who had authority."

Now here is a gem that will thrill you (*Luke 6:40*). A student is not above his teacher, but everyone fully trained will be like his Teacher!

4. Encouraging, exhorting (Rom 12:8)

Barnabas had this gift (*Acts 4:36*), as well as that of a teacher. *Acts 11:23, 26* says: "He was glad and encouraged them all to remain true to the Lord with all their hearts, He was a good man, full of the Holy Spirit and faith. So for a whole year Barnabas and Paul met with the church and taught great numbers of people."

For your further study the following are exciting scriptures: *2 Timothy 4:2; Hebrews 3:13, 10:25; 1 Peter 5:12; 2 Corinthians 5:20; Acts 16:40, 9:31*. For example, *Acts 15:32:* "Judas and Silas, who themselves were prophets, said much to encourage and strengthen the brethren." Do you see that a teacher like Barnabas or prophets like Judas and Silas can still be encouragers?

5. Generous giving (Rom 12:8)

This gift is a ministry of giving, but all Christians should be strong in this gift. Those who have this gift have discovered that the real blessing starts when you give more than a tenth of your gross income to God. The tithe is the Lord's, so it is the extra love offerings that enable God to pour out his blessing. Some scriptures to study are: *Malachi 3:8–11; Matthew 6:20, 33, 23:23; Mark 4:20; Luke 6:38; 2 Corinthians 9:5–15; 1 Corinthians 16:1; 2 Deuteronomy 8:18*.

Then there is the other side; the giving of oneself (*Mk 10:29–31*). "No one who has left home ... for Me and the Gospel, will fail to receive a hundred times as much."

Generous givers mostly live frugally in order to give more. *Proverbs 22:8* is useful in this regard: "A generous man will himself be blessed, for he shares his food with the poor." Giving must be in the faith that God will multiply the seed sown which will return as a harvest in countless ways. All are called to give in this way, but to some it will be their chief ministry. Give as if you are giving seed and by faith expect a harvest. We don't please God without faith.

6. Leadership (Rom 12:8)

Leadership means to lead, organise and take responsibility willingly. The one with this gift sees the overall picture, knows where he is going, sets goals for himself and those with him and has the inward drive to get it done. If it is a church, he sees everyone as having a ministry and motivates them to get started in their God-given gift.

New challenges always meet anyone with this gift. Is there a scriptural illustration of such a man? Yes there is: Nehemiah got directions from God (*Neh 1:4–11*). *Nehemiah 2:1–6* says that he even influenced the king. A person with this gift often breathes a "quick prayer to the God of heaven" (*Neh 2:4*) and gets flash answers! The result was that Nehemiah was given a job that could have taken many years – rebuilding the wall of Jerusalem – which he completed in 52 days! (*Neh 6:15–16*).

7. Mercy, comforting cheerfully (Rom 12:8)

Radiating the love of God, giving words of wisdom and comfort, cheerfully. Those with this gift are tender-hearted and full of compassion. Jesus is the supreme example as we see in *Matthew 9:36; 14:14:* "He had compassion on them and healed their sick." In our day, Mother Teresa expresses this gift beautifully. She lived among the dying in the streets of Calcutta and became a living expression of God's love, yet her need to withdraw and be alone with God was as important as her work.

Study *James 2:13:* "Judgement without mercy will be shown to anyone who has not been merciful." This proves the point that we should all move into all these gifts though we will especially excel in a few. *James 3:17* tells us that with God's wisdom we will be "pure, then peace loving, considerate, submissive, full of mercy and good fruit." The story of the good Samaritan is in *Luke 10:25–37; Ephesians 2:4* tells us: "God who is rich in mercy, because of His great love for us."

We all need to increase our percentage of this gift. Mercy helps people in trouble even though they don't deserve it.

8. Love (1 Peter 4:8; Romans 12:9, 10)

The Greek word is *Agape*, which means Divine love. God's love is imparted by faith and is kindled inside by the Holy Spirit. This is never *phileo*, our natural love, or *"eros"*, passionate love. This is the kind of love that *never fails* (*1 Cor 13:8*). God's love is not an emotional feeling, and is commanded by Jesus, as we read in *John 15:12*. "My commandment is this: Love each other as I have loved you."

This is not unfair, as God's love is an imparted love to be received, and is shed abroad in our inner being by the Holy Spirit (*Rom 5:5*). This is the love that will bring us to complete unity and let the world know that God sent Jesus, and that the Father loves you and me as much as He loves Jesus. (*John 17:23*).

Phileo love is the love you are born with. It will always fail. Its strength is not sufficient to keep a marriage from falling apart. *Agape* love you are never born with, as it is the God-given kind of love. You have to receive it from God and even then it is fairly easy to drop down to the level of *phileo* love. It might be as easy as an automatic gear change! To remain in the higher *agape* love, we have to affirm its presence in words by making this confession:

"Jesus commanded me to operate in God's love. I have it by faith and it is poured out into my heart by the Holy Spirit, dominating my life. *1 Corinthians 13:4–8* will be a reality in me. God's love in me is patient and kind. It does not envy, it does not boast and is not proud. It is not self-seeking, is not easily angered and keeps no record of wrongs. *Agape* love in me does not delight in evil, but rejoices with the truth. It will always protect, always trust, always hope and always persevere. This God kind of love in me will never fail!'"

If only couples planning on divorce would receive God's love by faith and begin to make this love real by making this confession together, their marriage would be saved. The trauma to the entire family could be averted.

9. Spiritual fervour, fervent in spirit, spiritual enthusiasm (Rom 12:11)

This is the short word *Zeo*, which means to be earnest and full of zeal as a result of the born again-spirit.

Apollos is said to have spoken with great spiritual fervour (*Acts 18:25*). This is the opposite to spiritual lethargy, and God's cure for laziness. It is Holy Spirit energy flowing through you. One man stands out in his exercise of this gift, the world evangelist with a special call to Africa, Reinhard Bonnke.

10. Joyful in hope (Rom 12:12)

Hope brings joy in the morning. Hope anticipates with pleasure and confidence. Hope is not faith, but is always a forerunner of faith. *Hebrews 11:1*: "Now faith is being sure of what we hope for." Hope gives you the vision and desire for things you take by faith. Then hope continues to assist in keeping you in faith to the known will of God, until you receive what you have prayed for.

Faith without hope is faithless! These three things will remain for eternity: Faith, hope and love. I am glad hope is a motivational gift that can be received, aren't you? *Romans 15:13* says: "May the God of hope fill you with all joy and peace as you trust in Him, so that you may overflow with hope by the power of the Holy Spirit."

11. Patience in affliction and tribulation (Rom 12:12)

Patience and perseverance go together. Affliction and tribulation never refer to sickness, but rather to other kinds of trouble; but here is good news. Jesus said according to *John 16:33*: "In this world you will have trouble, but take heart I have overcome the World!" Because of Jesus' victory, we too can be overcomers. This much is clear from *1 John 4:4*: "You, dear children, are from God and have overcome them, (every evil spirit) because the One who is in you is greater than the one who is in the world" (the devil).

You and I can resist the devil in the name of Jesus and he will flee from us (*James 4:7*). This makes me patient in trouble and free from oppression from the enemy.

12. Faithful in prayer to be an intercessor (Rom 12:12)

The King James version reads "instant in prayer". It means to be faithful, serving with diligence in prayer. It means never giving up, being courageous against the enemy, and fully co-operating with the Holy Spirit as He uses you as a prayer channel.

I always thought that there had to be a gift like this. God is raising an army of intercessors such as has never been seen before. With many it is their chief motivational gift. If we score low in this area and we will to pray in tongues, we can quickly move up to a score of more than 50 %. Start as you open your eyes, while still in bed. Pray as you walk to the kitchen to make you and your wife a cup of tea or coffee, pray as you read your Bible, as you go to work by bus or car.

Be like Paul. He prayed as he worked, making tents for the Roman army. That is how he claimed to be a champion as we see in *1 Corinthians 14:18*: "I thank God that I speak (pray) in tongues more than all of you." Paul majored in many areas of these motivational gifts. Through faith, we can improve in many of these gifts. Both my pastor, Ed Roebert, and I started in tongues by using the authority of *Mark 16:17*. As believers we used the authority of Jesus' name to speak out in new tongues. Why do I stress this? Because it takes the sweat out of prayer. It becomes easy and enables one to be faithful in prayer. In intercession you are dealing with the unknown; but the Holy Spirit knows everything and his words flow through you as you pray in tongues.

Someone who had a near-death experience saw heaven. He saw Jesus who told him that intercession in tongues on earth is now greater than at any time in history and is causing the river of life to rise quickly to flood level. When this happens, the Father will open the flood gates, and this will start the great end-time revival on earth. Some of the gates have already been opened. Our church has experienced the end time revival for three years now.

Today we would call someone who is faithful in prayer an intercessor. To be an intercessor means that this is one of the Father's special gifts to you. Cherish it!

13. Practice hospitality (Rom 12:13)

The whole verse says: "Share with God's people who are in need. Practice hospitality." *1 Peter 4:9–10* puts it this way: "Offer hospitality to one another without grumbling. Each one should use whatever gift he has received to serve others, faithfully administering God's grace in its various forms." This refers to the same gifts as in Romans 12.

What does hospitality mean? I looked up its meaning in Thayers and this is the gist of the meaning of the word: to show kindness and love to others, even strangers. To open your home and, if necessary, to put them up for the night. It is not necessary to prepare a banquet. It is sharing what you have. To some of you it will become your chief motive gift, and God has a great reward for you!

14. To bless others (Rom 12:14)

"Bless those who persecute you; bless and do not curse." Before we came to the Lord, the first thing we carelessly uttered was a curse. Now it is a blessing. The devil's way is to curse. God's way is to bless.

Pope John Paul II went to the prison especially to bless the man who shot him. He took him by the hand and said "I forgive you from the depths of my heart".

In *1 Chronicles 16:2* (KD) we read: "Blessed all the people in the name of the Lord". This is what Jesus wants us to do.

15. Empathy (Rom 12:15)

"Rejoice with those who rejoice; mourn with those who mourn" is how our text puts it. This is what empathy toward others means. A good dictionary might have something like this:

(1) It is the capacity to appreciate, even experience the emotions of others. Those with empathy don't slap you on the back and tell you to snap out of it. They bring you up to a point where you rejoice with their strength of spirit.

(2) Have you ever bought a new car and tried to show it off to friends, but they didn't notice it? They did not have empathy.

(3) To have this gift is to be like a cork riding the waves. The weather may be rough, but this gift enables you to bring others out on top with you.

16. Live in harmony with one another (Rom 12:16)

To live in strife is hell on earth; but to live in harmony is heaven on earth. The King James Bible says "Be of the same mind". The Living Bible: "Work happily together." The filling with the Holy Spirit is the key. *Ephesians 5:18–20* says: "Be continuously filed with the Holy Spirit and controlled by Him ... Sing and make music in your heart to the Lord ... Submitting to one another out of reverence for Christ."

In *Philemon 4:2* Paul pleads with Euodia and Syntyche to "agree with each other in the Lord". In these days of increasing love and unity, some of our best friends can be from other denominations. In my prison work, when I meet some of my Dutch Reformed, Anglican, Catholic and Methodist friends, our faces just light up with joy at meeting one another again.

I was speaking in a Catholic church once when one of the priests came up and hugged me and said "I love you, Father Jack." That was something special! I walked tall after that.

17. Humbleness and humility (Rom 12:16)

"Do not be proud, but be willing to associate with people of low position", says this verse. The Jerusalem Bible is even more down to earth: "Treat everyone with equal kindness; never be condescending but make friends with the poor." Humility is the opposite of pride, isn't it?

1 Peter 5:5 says: "Clothe yourself with humility toward one another because God opposes the proud but gives grace to the humble." Humility is not a matter of self-effort. It is only through faith that we have to clothe ourselves with God's gift.

18. Do not take revenge (Rom 12:17–21)

This whole passage says: "Do not repay evil for evil. Be careful to do what is right in the eyes of everybody. Live at peace with everyone as much as possible. Do not take revenge, my friends, but leave room for God's wrath, for it is written: 'It is mine to avenge; I will repay,' says the Lord."

This must be very important, as God puts it so strongly. How is one normally motivated before becoming a Christian? "I will get you for that!" is the usual retort, isn't it? As Christians we know that our Father can handle anyone, so always give the matter over to Him.

19. Speaking gracious words of God

1 Peter 4:11, "If anyone speaks he should do it as one speaking the very words of God." This can apply to preaching or to ordinary conversation. It means that the Holy Spirit can guide us in coversation and counselling as well.

Don't you think that Jesus was guided by the Holy Spirit in ordinary conversation? I am sure He was, so that Jesus is our role model. *Colossians 3:16* urges us, "Let the word of Christ dwell in you richly."

Why nineteen motivational gifts?

I am well aware that most students limit the number of motivational gifts to seven, and I think I understand why. When one reads *Romans 12*, one notices that the mood changes from statements in verse 8 to commands in verse 9, like "love must be sincere".

The thinking behind this is as follows: You have been gifted with the seven motivational gifts, therefore carry out the instructions from verse 9. It was meditation on *1 Peter 4:7–11* that led me to think differently. Let us read this scripture carefully: "The end of all things is near. Therefore be clear minded and self-controlled so that you can pray. Above all, love each other deeply, because love covers over a multitude of sins. Offer hospitality to one another without grumbling. Each one should use whatever gift he has received to serve others, faithfully administering God's grace in its various forms. If anyone speaks, he should do it as one speaking the very words of God. If anyone serves, he should do it with the strength God provides, so that in all things God may be praised through Jesus Christ. To him be the glory and the power for ever and ever. Amen."

Verse 7 expresses a similar thought to *Romans 12:2* which emphasises, "Be transformed by the renewing of your mind. Then you will be able to approve what God's will is." This to me is similar to *1 Peter 4:7*: "be clear-minded and self-controlled." In either case we cannot be "renewed in our minds" or "clear-minded" without our way of thinking being corrected by God's Word, and our minds being controlled by the Holy Spirit.

Romans 8:6 says: "The mind controlled by the Spirit is life and peace." Now look at *1 Peter 4:10*. The word "gift" is the same Greek word as in *Romans 12:6*. "Charisma" singular and "charismata" plural. So Peter is speaking about the same gifts as Paul.

The question is, does Peter speak about two gifts or four? In *1 Peter 4:10*, the Greek meaning of the word "manifold" in the King James Bible is, "extremely diverse", many and varied, abundant. The words "extremely diverse" indicate that there are not just a few of these motive gifts. On looking up the word "diverse", my dictionary says, differing, distinct, varying, multi-formed. This is in keeping with our Father's character, isn't it?

Now regarding the context in which Peter writes, do the words love and hospitality have anything to do with the gifts he mentions? I think they do, as verse 10 does not introduce a new subject. Peter is already speaking about gifts. He does not claim to mention them all, but talks as if motivational gifts were well-known in the early church. He then goes on to mention two more:

(1) Speaking in conversation as if you are speaking words of God.

(2) Serving. What is also significant is that the very same Greek words are used in Romans 12. Divine love, hospitality and serving. This is what leads me to believe that love and hospitality are also gifts. If this is so, it makes all the others gifts too. Here in 1 Peter 4 four gifts are mentioned. All four are repeated in Romans 12 where eighteen are mentioned. Love is then mentioned by Peter as a gift. This is how the break-through came to see that there are more than seven gifts mentioned in Romans 12.

Love is usually regarded as a fruit, and this is scripturally correct. Now we see it is also a gift. Love as a fruit takes a long time to ripen and mature in our lives. There are times when you can't wait that long. Your marriage is falling apart and now you need a quick infusion of God's love to change things. You need this love as God's gift! On another occasion you are faced with a drug addict or a person dying of AIDS and you know you need to show the compassion that Jesus showed, but your whole person is in rebellion. What can you do? Help is at hand in the form of God's gift of love. Quick as a flash you receive a new infusion of God's gift of love and you notice a change taking place inside which enables you to cope with this new situation.

How will I know what my special motive gifts are?

Just remember that these gifts enrich our lives and make us more like Christ. The saying "First I wanted the gifts, now I want the Giver" seems spiritual; but "spurn the gift and you spurn the Giver" is a true word. In *1 Corinthians 14:1* God's word tells us to "eagerly desire spiritual gifts". They always enrich our lives.

You say to me, "Brother Jack, how can I find out what my motive gift is?" It will be something you like to do. It will give you fulfilment. Talk it over with the Holy Spirit. After all, He is inside you. Listen to what He says in your thought pattern. Then try out that motivational gift. If you enjoy doing it that could be your main gift. There will be one main gift, but also some complementary ones, where you will score fairly high as well. God bless you!

Selwyn Hughes has written a small, but very helpful, book on the subject called *Discovering your place in the body of Christ*, published by Marshal Morgan and Scott. Try and get a copy.

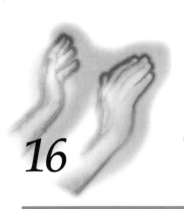

16

How will the gifts operate in my life?

I have listened to some of the world's great expositors of the gifts of the Holy Spirit, and I am thrilled! I now feel more eager than ever for the gifts to operate in my life. What can I do about it? It doesn't help me much if I am told "these things just happen, don't ask me how". If there is such a mystery about how to move into the gifts, it doesn't help me as an average Christian, does it?

I asked the Lord if there was a way to explain to other Christians how to start operating in the gifts, assuming that they fulfil the condition of longing for them. I believe the Lord has given me the answer to my question.

Remove every bias

You will notice that the "prayer language" heads the list of the gifts of the Spirit. I believe that this is God's order. I am not saying it is the greatest, but it is usually the first gift received. Don't be biased against the gift. I am going to assume that if you were biased against "tongues", you will now sincerely repent to God for being against one of his gifts. It follows that, if you dislike the gift, this dislike will carry over to the Giver. This hampers your crowning the Giver as Lord of all.

Some of you still can't get over your bias against "tongues". Perhaps this illustration will help you. An engagement party is in progress. Now comes the great moment that everybody has been waiting for. The young man is going to place the engagement ring on his fiancée's finger. He holds up the large, sparkling diamond as he takes the ring out of the velvet-lined box. Cries of approval are heard round the room. It is a beautiful gift, fit for a queen. There is only one thing that can mar the great occasion: The beautiful young girl refuses the gift. Everybody is embarrassed, to say the least. What does it mean? Just this, that by spurning the gift, the young girl is spurning the giver.

You may have questions about the gifts, and these, of course, you may ask the Lord. Even these questions are more easily answered if you have the "prayer language". The answers can come so easily by the second gift, that of "interpretation". More correctly, "replication", as through this gift God replies to you.

You see, it all comes back to the "prayer language". I believe you have come to the point where you can say, "I'm sorry Lord that I even questioned some of your gifts. Forgive me." God bless you as you are released to be the person God wants you to be. You are now pleasing God by faith (*Hebrews 11:6*).

If we have reservations about one of God's gifts, we cannot have faith in it. God's Word says, "Everything that does not come from faith is sin" (*Rom 14:23*). Praise God, we prefer the way of faith.

In the 1970's some of my fellow deacons and I were praying together on a Saturday afternoon during a half-day of prayer. We were asking the Lord at one point why we were so impoverished in all the gifts and whether God meant us to have all the gifts, or only some of them. Shortly after, there was a "prayer language" as the Holy Spirit gave utterance. This released the following prophecy or reply from God:

"I have already given you all the gifts of My Holy Spirit, but in every situation you must listen for My voice. I am speaking to you now in response to the cry from your spirits through the Holy Spirit. I will give you specific instructions to suit every situation. This will be to you a Word of knowledge, covered by My wisdom so that you will be enabled to do My works.

"You must take up the authority I have given you, and you will begin doing the miracles and works I have done. I declare to those of you who are fearful of My gifts that I have not given you the spirit of fear, but of power, of love, and a sound mind. You shall enter the operation of My gifts in your life by faith."

This put an end to our impoverishment! This is God's answer as to how we can receive his gifts for his glory, and how we can do what Jesus did.

A practical experience

I had driven five long hours after having been away from home for five days, and had just arrived home when the telephone rang. It was my friend Don Griesel, the housemaster of one of the boarding schools in a small town 175 km from Pretoria.

"Jack, will you come over and help me?" he asked. Normally I am only too pleased to move into the gift of "Helps". I said to him, "Don, I am so tired. Can I come in the morning?" He replied, "I have brought two of my students to Pretoria and I have promised Johan's mother that I would take him back early tomorrow. I want you to pray with me that God will lengthen his leg which has been short from birth."

This gave me a shock. Short from birth! His mother said she did not believe in healing of this kind and that people should be left as God created them. I now phoned the prayer chain, as I felt weak and in a panic.

The chain works like this: One phones the leader at once, who prays with you, and then he phones another, so that in a short time one has thirty people praying in real support. I could feel these prayers taking effect as the fatigue left me and courage was restored.

I got a further shock when I saw how small and under-developed the muscles in Johan's right leg were. The leg itself was two inches shorter than the other. Let it be said, to Johan's credit, that he had become the school's champion high-jumper, using only his left leg. Three weeks before he had trusted Christ as his Saviour. It was a great encouragement for him to learn that his hero, Reinardt Shiel, the Springbok high-jumper and an all-Africa record holder at 2.26 m was also a fine Christian. He is a member of Sportsmen for Christ.

Well, as we began praying and holding Johan's legs, nothing happened. We commanded his right leg to lengthen, using Jesus' name. Nothing happened. The three of us agreed to praise the Lord in prayer, as He answers in the praises of his people.

Still nothing happened. Now we had done all we could. I then said to Don, "I am stumped. Let us use the prayer language and ask the Lord what we must do." We did and a vision began to form of Johan's spine. I tried to blank it off, as I wanted to see the leg. Again the vision formed and then I could see an X-ray of the lower vertebrae curving to the right side. I began to tell my colleagues what I had seen, and they began to see the same thing. Then the vision became clearer. It wasn't the leg that was shorter, but the curved spine which was lifting the hip joint. We had been praying for the wrong thing.

The vision then changed. Now I could see the nervous system and a chain of nerves leading from the spine to each leg. The network of nerves to the left leg was very strong; that to the right leg was very weak. The Lord was saying, "Now you see the problem." I told the others exactly what I had seen, and they saw the same. Without my knowing it I was giving out a "Word of Knowledge". This led to faith in all our hearts, the "gift of faith".

Now we knew exactly what to do. I placed my hand on Johan's spine and in the name of Jesus commanded the spine to straighten out and the discs to build up on the side where they were so thin. Johan called out, "Uncle, look, my knee is moving!" We looked and were just in time to see the sudden movement of the knee. We excitedly measured the legs. They were equal. How we praised the Lord!

The second prayer was to command the creation of a strong nervous system in the right leg, in the name of Jesus. This also happened and the proof is that over the years, the muscles of Johan's right leg have gone on developing with exercise.

The appraisal of what the Lord did

We sat down, praising the Lord and analysing what had happened. We had been somewhat embarrassed since we had wanted to help a newly-born Christian, but at first nothing had taken place. We had been about to stop there, and to tell Johan to keep on trusting that his leg would eventually come right. His mother would then have said, "I told you so". Suddenly, we had found a key.

Instead, we had got on to the "hot line" to God *who knows*. We have the privilege of asking for an interpretation, for God has told us that we may ask. *1 Corinthians 14:13* says: "For this reason the man who speaks in a tongue should pray that he may interpret what (God) says." I have altered one word. It is not what we say that we will understand, but what God says back to us.

The Greek word for interpretation is *hermeneuo*. The verb means "to explain, make clear, give utterance to, give expression and power of speech to." Thayer's gives the following definition:

"Verb form. To explain in words, expound or interpret. Interpretation of what was spoken in obscurity." This is derived from the noun *Hermes*. The translators all seem to have the idea that the gift of interpretation is interpreting what was said to God in tongues.

This is not the case. It is to explain or to give utterance to God's reply to us. It is to give expression and power of speech to a person of what God says back to us. The gift of Replication, that is, power to reply, would be a more accurate word to explain what actually takes place.

In *2 Samuel 5:19* David enquired of the Lord, "Shall I go and attack the Philistines? Will you hand them over to me?" The Lord answered him immediately: "Go, for I will surely hand the Philistines over to you.". It is always important to receive God's reply. When David conferred with each of his officers (*1 Chronicles 13:1*), the result was disaster. A man was killed, and the whole project of bringing back the ark was abandoned. It was God's work done man's way. The project could only be continued when they found out how God wanted it done (*1 Chronicles 15:2*). Only the Levites were allowed to carry the ark of God.

What do we learn from this? Was David able to get a more direct answer from the Lord than the New Testament Christian? Can we receive guidance from the Lord moment by moment as David did in the battle? Could it be that we are not doing things the way God wants for the New Testament Christian?

The prayer language is the one gift where we are given full control

We can start and stop the prayer language at will. We can pray as much as we like or withhold prayer in the spirit with our wills. In fact, that we should pray in the spirit is a command as we see in *Ephesians 6:18*: "Pray in the spirit on all occasions."

The gift of interpretation is one we can ask for, but we do not control it

We do not have full control over the gift of interpretation (replication), but we have the privilege of asking for it, as we have seen in *1 Corinthians 14:13*. The Holy Spirit will come back with God's answer in the way He knows best. In the case we are analysing, his direction came in two visions as well as in words. The Holy Spirit is in complete control, but He only replies according to our faith. I simply told the others what I had seen. Was that another gift in operation? Yes, it was. It was the Word of Knowledge, that is to say, a fragment of God's knowledge imparted to his children in the form of a vision. As soon as the others heard the description, they saw the vision as well.

This had a dramatic effect on all of us. We were no longer in the dark. We could see exactly what the trouble was and suddenly faith rose in our hearts. Another gift was being given by the Holy Spirit – the gift of faith. Now we could pray with authority, without doubt, and the next gift came into operation – working of miracles. This was immediate before our eyes. Next we prayed for the nervous system. There was probably a slower healing of the nerves of the right leg. It is fair to say that another gift was in operation – the gifts of healing. After several years now, the development of the muscles in the right leg is proof that the nervous system was healed as well.

Isn't this so wonderful! Six gifts came into operation by asking the Lord for an interpretation. Now here is an explanation of the word "interpretation" I had never thought of before.

Interpretation, the Greek word *hermeneuo* and its true meaning

At one time Paul was called *Hermes*. "Paul they called Hermes because he was the chief speaker" (*Acts 14:12*). Hermes was a mythological god who was the messenger and interpreter of all the other gods. They were so far removed from the people that Hermes gathered the messages from the gods and flew down to earth. He would then whisper what the gods wanted to say into the ears of receptive people. Here is the whole point of *hermeneuo*. What the God Hermes did was *hermeneuo*.

When Paul wanted to tell us about the gift we now call interpretation, he gave us the word *hermeneuo*. This is the picture. When we pray in tongues, the Bible tells us in *1 Corinthians 14:2:* "We do not speak to men but to God. Indeed no one (but God) understands him; he utters mysteries (secret words) with his spirit."

Now when you ask God for an interpretation, you get what Hermes did. You receive a reply from God, in answer to what your spirit said to God, in words given by the Holy Spirit. *Hermeneuo* is God replying to you.

Imagine a gift of the Spirit which enables you to hear from God more clearly! Don't we often struggle and wonder if and when God is speaking to us? Here is a gift that will help us to be sure! When we might have a suspicion that God wants to communicate with us, or when we want direction from God, what should we do? Why not pray softly in tongues and then say, "Lord, please speak back to me in the gift of interpretation." Then believe that the next thing that pops into your mind in thought form is God. It can come to the mind in thought words or in picture form.

David got thought words to his mind when he asked God if he should go up and fight the Philistines. Habakkuk said in *Habakkuk 2:1:* "I will look to see what God will say to me." He heard from God in picture or vision form. Just because we are God's children we can hear from God. God can even speak to those who are not his children. Looking back, wasn't He speaking to you? Yes, no doubt we can hear or see God's voice as well as David or Habakkuk. Now we can go one step further, for there is a gift we should be using to enable us to hear from God more clearly! The gift we call interpretation or *hermeneuo*. Use it!

The gift of "helps"

There is a small gift from Jesus that no one seems to take much notice of. That is the gift of "Helps", or simply being a helper. Yet this is a key gift. If you do not long to help others you can hardly be said to have an outgoing spirit. It means that you are probably self-centred. If this description fits you, then you have not experienced the liberty with which Christ makes us free.

"Helps" comes from the Greek word: *antilepsis*. The verb form means, "to lay hold of, to take part with, to assist someone else". I think we could use the word "assistant". Would you like to be the Holy Spirit's assistant? John Mark started out as a helper: "John was with Paul and Barnabas as their helper" (*Acts 13:5*). Had he not started out as a missionary helper, I wonder if he would have been chosen to write part of the Bible? That is, the Gospel according to Mark.

Who are we really helping? God Himself, by helping his people. *Hebrews 6:10* tells us: "God is not unjust; He will not forget your work and the love you have shown Him as you have helped His people and continue to help them."

Isn't it a wonderful privilege to help God and to express your love to Him because you help his people? If so far you have no inclination to be a "help", this is the point at which you ought to start.

Let us assume that you begin by being a helper. To gain experience, be a helper to someone who is experienced in the field you want to work in for the Lord. This is not essential, of course, but desirable.

To summarise what God did for Johan:

1. First, there was a willingness on our part to be a "help!"
2. Prayer language or "hot line" to ask God for the answer.
3. Interpretation – God speaking back.
4. Vision – to make the answer clearer.
5. Word of knowledge – communicating to others what God said.
6. Gift of faith arising from God's knowledge.
7. Gift of miracles.
8. Gift of healings.

Is this a pattern we can use for ourselves in the Lord's work? I'm sure it is.

Let us assume that the next case – counselling – is quite different. We still need the Holy Spirit's gifts.

Steps in putting the gifts to practical use

1. Helper: We are willing to minister to the needs of the person, but we don't know what to say.
2. Prayer language: "Hot line" to the Father.

3. Interpretation: God speaks in words to your mind and tells you to ask the person, "Do you think that you will go to heaven when you die?"

4. The above question is a Word of Wisdom. The person answers "I hope so". This opens out the conversation and you can lead him to the Lord.

Let us consider another imaginary case.

1. Helper. You are willing. Something worries you about this case. You keep talking and listening.

2. At the same time you softly use the prayer language.

3. You ask for an interpretation (*1 Cor 14:13*).

4. The Holy Spirit comes back with the gift "discerning of spirits". You know now that the person is bothered with evil spirits. You are guarded in your language. You say, "Somewhere along the line you have given a foothold to the devil. Let us pray together and ask the Lord to show us what it is."

Let me explain here that we are not talking about demon possession. The Greek speaks of "demonization". Christians can be attacked by the devil, too, especially when they have given the devil a foothold by their slow repentance.

Deal scripturally with the trouble first. Explain *Exodus 34:6–7* and show how the devil may possibly have obtained a hold on us legally because of what our forefathers did. The blood of Jesus has the power to remove any sin, even from previous generations, but not automatically. We have to ask the Lord to apply its cleansing and delivering power from the sins of the past and the present to our lives and so eliminate every foothold the devil has secured.

All resentment, rebellion, contact with the occult or with the signs of the zodiac, foretelling of the stars, fortune-tellers, teacups, palm-reading, and any spirit of unforgiveness toward anyone must be confessed and forgiven. This is so that you can retrieve all ground given to the devil.

Firstly, in accordance with *Matthew 18:18*, bind the devil in the name of Jesus Christ. Secondly, release the person from the devil's clutches. Then, on the authority of *James 4:7*, let him make a full commitment to Jesus as Lord. Then ask him to command the devil to be gone in the name of Jesus. The devil attacks many times. Every new attack must be met with a strong command to the devil to go in the authority of the name of Jesus.

Fail here, and all one does is invite the devil to take hold on you again. A choice must be made whether you are totally committed to Christ or partly committed to the enemy and partly to self.

The final need is to be filled and baptised with the Holy Spirit in faith.

5. Should the Holy Spirit want to communicate, you should be ready to receive a "Word of Knowledge" to enable you to discern whether there are other points of contact with the enemy not yet dealt with.

An actual case of healing

During a weekend visit to a church, a number of people were baptised with the Holy Spirit on the Saturday night. After the Sunday morning service, I felt led by the Lord to invite those who had been baptised with the Holy Spirit the evening before to volunteer to become God's "helpers" and to pray for the sick. The ladies prayed for the ladies, and the men for men. I did not pray for anyone.

I said, "You folk already have one gift of the Holy Spirit, and that is the prayer language. Now you are going to move into other gifts as the Holy Spirit guides you. Not one of you will ask these people what ails them. We will ask the Lord. We will do this by silently praying in the prayer language, and the Father will reply in one of three ways:

1. In words coming from the spirit to the mind;
2. In a vision which will indicate what the problem is and what to pray for;
3. The Lord may give you the same pain the person has and you will know what to pray for.

These are some ways in which God communicates the "word of knowledge".

After two minutes one lady said, "I see what appears to be a green sac on the right side of the tummy. The pain is severe." I thought it must be the gall bladder. Another had a vision of much phlegm and congestion in the upper region of the chest. A third had a vision of a great roughness of the bones inside the knee joints. I thought, arthritis. These were all symptoms present in the same woman.

As the women gave "words of knowledge" on the visions they saw, faith rose in all our hearts, especially when the woman confirmed that these three things had been a problem for years.

Each person prayed for the part he or she saw in the vision. The pain ceased on the right side, breathing became free and the person could move her knees freely without pain. I saw her three months later and she showed me how easily she could use her knees.

The men were praying elsewhere, and one man said, "I have suddenly got a pain on the side of my right eye. Is God speaking to me?" I said, "I think so. The proof will be when you ask the man who is being prayed for." This "word of knowledge" proved to be quite right; it was the man's right eye which was painful. He was also healed.

These people had never prayed for the sick before. What was the secret of their success? The gifts of the Holy Spirit operating through them. Miracles and healing come easily when the gift of faith is operating. This is not our faith, nor is it the fruit of faith built up over the years. When the person heard the "word of knowledge" which fitted in with his exact complaint, he received the gift of faith at the same time.

Fellow Christians, this works. It's exciting! It's what God is doing today! This is not focusing attention on a great central figure who is doing miracles and you must be prayed for by him or else you will not be healed. This is training God's people to do God's work in God's way. It is the ministry of Christ's body.

I somehow feel that some of you have not yet got the confidence to allow the Holy Spirit to use you as He would like. He will not force you. He will only gently nudge you to start being a helper to others. I hope by now you have learned how to confess the good things God says about you so that you may correct the low image you may have of yourself.

Now I want to tell you something we should be shouting from the house-tops! This will make you eager to go. It is a gem from the Word of God that I have missed most of my life, but it has been there all the time. It has given me greater confidence than ever before in my desire to be a "help". The next chapter will tell you more about this.

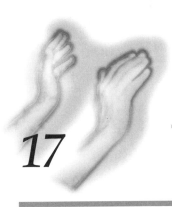

Deliverance from the curse of the law

17

Deliverance from the law

Turn to *Galatians 3:13:* "Christ redeemed us from the curse of the law by becoming a curse for us, for it is written 'Cursed is everyone who is hung on a tree' (the cross)."

To find out exactly what this means, we have to turn to the Old Testament where both blessings and curses are set forth clearly.

First the blessings: *Deuteronomy 28:1* says: "If you fully obey the Lord your God ...

v. 2 All these blessings will come upon you ...

v. 3 You will be blessed in the city and blessed in the country.

I like this, don't you? Let us glance at some of the other verses to see what sort of blessings belong to us!

v. 5 "Our food will be blessed." I want that, don't you?

v. 7 I want "my enemies to be defeated."

v. 8 I want "blessings ... on everything I put my hand to."

v. 11 I want to be blessed out of poverty and I want the "Lord to grant me abundant prosperity."

v. 12 I want the Lord "to open the heavens ... and to bless all the works of my hands."

The "Good News" from the New Testament is that we can have all these blessings because Jesus has bought them for us with his precious blood. Under the Old Covenant people had to make a special sacrifice for the times they had missed it and disobeyed God. *Romans 3:23* says: "We have all sinned and fall short of the glory of God" so we qualify for the curses set out in *Deuteronomy 28:15* onwards. These curses are devastating and make me shiver to think of them. I have actually endured many of them, even as a Christian. That is because I was ignorant of *Galatians 3:13*.

I knew Jesus had died to save me from sins and to bring me home to heaven. Christ died to deliver you and me from the curse of the law.

The old covenant, to put it mildly, was a terrible inconvenience. To be required to obey all those laws, ten major ones and 613 bylaws! Adam had only one law and he could not keep that one. I rejoice that I am not under the law now. By fulfilling the law, Jesus has taken all the burden of keeping all these laws away from us. I love Jesus for simplifying things. *Galatians 5:14* says "the entire law is summed up in a single command: 'Love your neighbour as yourself'."

"How will all this be a help to me in becoming a helper?" you ask. Well, reading the curses of *Deuteronomy 28*, we see what we have been delivered from.

This deliverance is not automatic anymore than our salvation is automatic. We have to receive deliverance. If we let the devil whip us, and put all sorts of diseases on us, the Lord will not say anything to the devil. We have to resist the devil (*Jas 4:7*). If we rise up strong in spirit, filled and baptised with the Holy Spirit's power, we can tell the devil that we are not having any of these curses, in the name of Jesus.

Why? Because "Jesus has redeemed us from the curse of the law." Since Jesus went to such pains to take the curse for us, we shall be guilty of gross ingratitude if we do not allow his work to be effective in us. What we would really be saying is that what Jesus did is not enough. Peter had this kind of feeling when Jesus was going to wash his feet. *John 13:8*: "'No', said Peter, 'you shall never wash my feet.' Jesus answered, 'unless I wash you, you have no part with Me.' 'Then, Lord,' Simon Peter replied, 'not just my feet but my hands and my head as well.'" Peter got the message and so should we. Jesus' work is perfect and complete. I think of one of the most important things He ever did for us was to take the curse of the law so that we do not need to bear it.

The curse of the law

Let us take a look at the severity of the curses outlined in *Deuteronomy 28:15* onwards, particularly with regard to sickness and disease and our deliverance from this curse of the law.

As we begin reading, it seems a pity that most translators put the blame on God for initiating them. *Deuteronomy 28:20–21* says "The Lord will send on you curses, confusion and rebuke in everything you put your hand to, until you are destroyed, and come to sudden ruin because of the evil you have done in forsaking Him. The Lord will plague you with diseases until you are destroyed."

When I read these words: "send on you", "plague you", "The Lord will afflict you" and particularly *Isaiah 45:7* "I create evil or disaster." My spirit says within me "This can't be right regarding my Heavenly Father. He can't be the author of evil."

I was so glad that Dr Robert Young, who compiled the exhaustive Young's concordance, said that these verbs translated as "send" (*Deuteronomy 28:20*) and "create evil" (*Isaiah 45:7*) are all in the permissive rather than the causative sense.

A more accurate translation of *Deuteronomy 28:15* would be: "The Lord will permit these curses to come on you, confusion and rebuke in everything you put your hand to." God permits evil, but is not the author of evil. Curses and evil come from the source of curses and evil, that is, the devil. I have changed the wording of my Bible accordingly as I do not believe in perpetuating mistakes which show my Heavenly Father in a bad light.

Deuteronomy 28:22, 29, 33, 47 says: "The Lord will allow you to be attacked with wasting disease, with fever, and inflammation, scorching heat and drought, with blight and mildew ... The sky over your head will be bronze, the ground beneath you iron. The Lord will allow you to be defeated before your enemies.

"The Lord will permit you to be afflicted with the boils of Egypt and with tumours, festering sores and the itch from which you cannot be cured. The Lord will allow you to be afficted with madness, blindness and confusion of the mind ... You will be unsuccessful in everything you do: ... Day after day you will be oppressed and robbed, with no one to rescue you ... You will have nothing but cruel oppression all your days ... Because you did not serve the Lord your God joyfully and gladly in the time of prosperity."

Deuteronomy 28:59, 61 reads: "The Lord will allow fearful plagues on you and your children, harsh prolonged disasters and severe lingering illnesses (like cancer) ... He will allow you to be assailed by every kind of sickness and disaster not recorded in this Book of the law until you are destroyed."

These must be the harshest words written in the Bible. Who wants all this? No one. Here is the Good News! We don't need to have any of these things because Christ took them upon Himself for us. *Galatians 3:13* tells us: "Christ redeemed us from the curse of (what we have just read) by becoming a curse for us."

Hallelujah! Thank you Jesus! I love you, Lord of my life.

This brings victory

Meditate on all this. It will bring healing to you and your loved ones. It is the most powerful message on healing I see in the Bible. It brings us healing from every possible kind of sickness.

It will enable us to prosper in whatever we put our hand to. Many of us will now have confidence to start out in our own business where God can really bless us.

For too long many of us have been the tail, instead of the head. Now you really will be God's helper in giving generously. Now you will pray for others with such confidence because you know Jesus has bought deliverance for you with his own precious blood from "every kind of sickness and even disaster not recorded in this book of the law".

Your new house or factory is not going to be burned down. The devil won't be able to do it as you will hold him to his defeat. Your car or home will not be broken into, your body will be victorious over germs and viruses because they die when the devil tries to put them on you. You are under a new law of the Spirit. "The law of the of the Spirit of life has set me free from the law of sin and death" (*Rom 8:2*).

Yes, the devil will be puzzled. He will say "I have prepared my most potent viruses and germs! My demons have been sent out to put them on those men and women doing greatest damage to my kingdom. I can't understand it. In the past they were so effective. Now these germs die instantly when they touch their bodies! I worked out the most perfect disasters to wipe out those Christian business men, but suddenly my demon spirits meet an army of great shining warriors who put my "strong men" to flight. Where I once had victory, now I have defeat. I get so mad because my forces flee in seven different directions. What is worse, they get bound with thongs by the angelic spirits who take them to desolate places where they cannot be used by me again. I don't know what I'm going to do, the pain from the bruising in my head is so bad!"

The ministry of angels

A few years ago a member of our church brought a friend to the evening service who was very sceptical of what she had heard about the renewal. The church was packed with more than 2 000 people, with more sitting outside. Well, God is always doing new things and the service was an unusual one. One hundred and twenty eight were baptised, and a large number came forward for salvation and the baptism of the Holy Spirit.

Towards the end of the service, the visitor leaned over to her friend and asked: "Do angels always go forward with all those people?" None of us had seen the angels, but God used a visitor to open our spiritual eyes to see what God is doing these days.

Could it be scriptural? Yes. *Hebrews 1:14* says, "Are not all angels ministering spirits sent to serve those who will inherit salvation?"

Friends, you have all the gifts of the Spirit at your disposal. You don't become as skilled in their use as is possible in the Holy Spirit, if you don't start out in faith. You have the angels helping you as God's ministering spirits. They are under God's personal direction. Don't brush them off through unbelief. Let us meditate before the Lord, find out where and how He wants us to start. Confess "I will get moving in the ministry He wants."

I don't mean full-time ministry. Don't give up your job because, "If you do not work you will not eat" (*2 Thess 3:10*). When you prove yourself in the ministry God gives, the church will recognise it and appoint you full-time. That is if it has a New Testament structure. Some, like Paul, supported himself. In prison ministry I also have to support myself.

The starting point is always moving into the gift of "helps". Be a Helper to the one who is the greatest Helper, the Holy Spirit. He needs you!

The ministry of "helps"

My great friend Arthur Morren, now gone to be with the Lord, was God's gift to me in helping me with the grammar, received the baptism of the Holy Spirit together with the following gift of worshipping, praising and praying in "tongues".

Arthur had been excommunicated from his church after having been with them most of his life. A few days after meeting him, he said to me, "I would love to hear God's voice, as I have never heard Him speak to me." Then he said, "I feel I should offer my services to help you with your book." I said, "Well, Arthur, you are hearing the Lord speak to you now as your help is my greatest need." You see, he was willing to move into the gift of "helps". After working on the book for some time, Arthur said, "I believe the Holy Spirit is speaking to me about Jesus baptising me with his Holy Spirit. Do you think I could move into his gifts?" I said, "Doubtless. Let's set the time and place. Sunday afternoon, at your house."

Arthur received the baptism with the accompanying gift of tongues. He spent half an hour praising God in the "prayer language". The following day he flew out to spend three weeks in England and Scotland. He said,

"What a blessing it will be to use this gift on the plane and while touring overseas, knowing that the Holy Spirit will be praying for everything in advance."

On Saturday afternoon, Joe Garlington from Mobile, Alabama, spoke to us about being God's "number two" man. Paul needed his Timothy, Moses needed Joshua, Elijah needed Elisha. Most people start off wanting to be a Paul or a Moses. God does not work that way. Let us start off just wanting to be a "help".

At this point Rita Strydom in our church was suddenly taken ill with a severe abdominal pain down the right side, and was hospitalised for diagnosis and treatment. Dr Danie Gouws of "Hatfield", who loves the Lord, having himself been healed of an incurable heart condition, did everything possible to discover the cause of Rita's illness. He prayed for her, and I prayed for her several times, and at one time she had relief from pain for about 36 hours. In the end she had to be discharged from the hospital as no organic cause could be found. She was in worse pain than before. Having heard she was home again and no better, I realised that Rita needed help fast. My friend Gordon Marran came with me to pray for her as she lay in pain. First, we asked the Lord how we should pray. I received a vision of a blackness over the right side, with five arrows piercing the body. I asked the Lord what it meant, and He said it was the work of the enemy.

We immediately took authority over the work of Satan in the name of Jesus. Then we asked the Lord to overwhelm her in the power of his Holy Spirit. As her body went limp, we asked our heavenly Father to reveal to Rita by his Spirit what had given the enemy the opening in her armour to inflict such harm. God gave Rita a fifteen-minute vision in which she seemed to relive some very difficult experiences in her life. We encouraged her not to fight off the vision, as the Holy Spirit was not making a mistake! I still don't know what she saw, but when the vision was over, the relief showed in her face. She said the vision had been like a film being projected onto a white wall.

We asked the Lord what we should do next. The arrows were gone, but the blackness remained. Then, using the authority of Jesus' name, we commanded the blackness and all pain to go. Immediately light flooded out the darkness and the pain was gone.

Let us analyse what actually happened. All Gordon and I did was to desire to be "helps". Twice we used the authority of the name of Jesus. Once we put a short request to our heavenly Father. The Holy Spirit did all the rest. I have never seen a counselling session more beautifully done. The

Holy Spirit showed a movie of the key points on the screen of her mind. He knew this vision was needed to bring about Rita's release. Why don't we allow the Holy Spirit to counsel people directly? His name is Counsellor. Let us move into God's modern methods.

The next day Rita was up and well. She said, "Now I am ready for the baptism with the Holy Spirit, and I am eager for the 'prayer language' too." After having longed for the experience for years, she was able to receive both very easily, without the laying on of hands.

The outpouring of God's Spirit has already commenced. We are living in the final, victorious age just before Christ's coming again. He needs millions of "helpers". Can you say no to Him when He needs you? Start now! The Holy Spirit is your Teacher and Guide. You need never be afraid. You are worth so much to Jesus.

Jesus wrote seven letters to seven churches in the Book of Revelation. Each one He ends with significant words: *"To him who overcomes I will give ..."* No one who reads this book can possibly become a lukewarm Christian, and have Jesus say to him as in *Revelation 3:16:* "I am about to spue you out of My mouth."

We will be of those that, "Have an ear" and who will "hear what the Spirit says to the Churches."

We will be "overcomers" (*Rev 3:21*) "Just as Jesus overcame." We will heed Jesus' words in *Luke 21:36:* "Be always on the watch, and pray that you may be able to escape all that is about to happen (speaking of the Great Tribulation) and that you will be able to stand before the Son of Man."

It is to "overcomers" Jesus is speaking when He says again in *Revelation 3:10:* "I will also keep you from the hour of trial to come upon the whole world to test those who live on the earth." Again, speaking of the Great Tribulation to take place after the victorious church has been snatched away to meet Jesus in the air, and go on with Him to heaven.

Jesus said in *Revelation 3:21:* "To him who overcomes I will give the right to sit with Me on My throne, just as I overcame and sat down with My Father on His throne." It's a massive throne big enough for *you!*

I have trusted God for 3 000 million souls in this imminent outpouring of God's Spirit before Jesus returns, and yet that is only a little more than half of the world's population. Jesus needs helpers to bring them in. I think Dr Justin Michel's short testimony he wrote after reading this manuscript and making valuable suggestions to me is important. This is what he said about his relationship between the Lord and himself:

"To me Christianity is simply a loving friendship between the Lord Jesus and myself. It starts with my realising that I am not good, but that Jesus loves me and that He is the only way to God. When I met Him, his love drew my heart to Himself. He forgave me and made me love and trust Him; knowing Him and his beauty has made me happy.

"He taught me that only my disobedience can spoil our friendship – and that when I sin I must admit it and say I'm sorry because it hurts Him – even to the shedding of his blood and this He clearly showed me on the Cross. In all this He makes me new again and the old self-love and self-trust give way as I learn to follow and love Him more and more. The Spirit of Jesus (the Holy Spirit) calls me to love Him with all my heart and to love others as myself, because He loves them even as He loves me. And He wants me to meet together with them; to read his book, and talk to Him often. He teaches me things and speaks in many ways into my heart which He seeks to fill completely and from which He strives to drive out all the remaining self-love. Because He is God, He has the right to ask me to yield all of my life and desires to Him so that our friendship can become perfect. He wants me to walk in the light as He is in the light and to live with Him in his house forever. But for now I want to be one of his helpers down here!"

I agree. Yes, I am determined to be one of Jesus' "helpers" here and now! Only in his strength of course. Are you?

You will, because God says in *Psalm 110:3:* "God's people will offer themselves willingly in the day of His power."

Will you?